FREEDOM III
Carnality, Denial and the Judgments of God

FREEDOM III
Carnality, Denial and the Judgments of God

The Investigation of True Repentance concludes...
by Ed Marr

Christian Literature & Artwork
A BOLD TRUTH Publication

Dedication

I thank my Heavenly Father, for His grace which, as a spiritual endowment, enabled me to fulfill His charge to me to write this investigation.

Unless otherwise indicated, Bible quotations are taken from the King James Version of the Bible. Copyright © 1988 by B. B. Kirkbride Bible Company, Inc.,

Thompson-Chain Reference Bible, 5th Improved Edition. Also, from the Amplified Bible. Copyright © 1987 by The Zondervan Corporation and the Lockman Foundation

The Strong's Exhaustive Concordance of the Bible. Copyright © 1990 by Thomas Nelson Publishers.

1st Printing
Volume One Repentance:
The Doctrine of God and The Knowledge of Salvation
Copyright © 2004 by Ed Marr
ISBN 1-594675-59-7

2nd Printing w/New Title and Revisions
FREEDOM III - Carnality, Denial and the Judgments of God
Copyright © 2015 by Ed Marr
ISBN 13: 978-0-9965908-8-4

Printed in the United States of America

Bold Truth Publishing
300 West 41st
Sand Springs, Oklahoma 74063
www.BoldTruthPublishing.com

All rights reserved solely by the author. The author guarantees all contents are original and do not infringe upon the legal rights of any other person or work. No part of this book may be reproduced in any form without the permission of the author.

The views expressed in this book are not necessarily those of the publisher.

Table of Contents

Author's Preface .... *i*
Introduction: The Birth of a Concept. 1

BOOK 1: FREEDOM
Chapter 1: Theological Concepts and Ideas 5
Man's Traditional Precepts 8
A Limited Grace Period is not an Age of Grace 12
The Age of Grace or the Age of Promiscuity 14
A Topical Investigation of Grace 15
The Nomenclature of Grace 16
Grace Applications 16
Contrast to/of Grace 21
Itemized Bipolarities of Grace 21
Church Distinctions 26
An Implanted Heart is a Saved Soul 27
Heaven's Court 31
Carnal Attitudes and Hostile Mind Sets 33
The Elements of Criminal and Civil Law 34
Iniquity is to a Guilty Mind 35
The Seventh Day 36
The Prophetic Word of Faith 40
There's a Warrant Out for Your Arrest! 42
The Call of Repentance 43
An Elementary Presumption 44
The Presumptive Heritage of the Church 45
Doing Time with 3 Hots and a Cot 48
A Prisoner of Jesus Christ 49

Chapter 2: Repentance In the Book of Genesis........................51
    He Shall Sever and His Wrath Shall Fall 51
    God Shall Set His Face Against the Crookedness of Man........55
    The Evidence Speaks for Itself 56
    Did God?..58
    We Must Regret Our Evil Activity 58
    A Lemon is not a Make of an Automobile 61
    Noah Found Grace 62
    One Choice is No Choice..62
    Repentance as a Memorial.......................................63

Chapter 3: Repentance In the Book of Exodus 65
    Freedom from Bondage 65
    The Violent Take it by Force...................................66
    Repentance at the Tabernacle...................................67
    A Tabernacle, Temple or a Shrine...............................68
    Types and Shadows..69
    Repentance as the Knowledge of Salvation.......................69
    The Urim and Thummin 71
    Long Standing Disobedience 72
    False Repentance 74
    Turning State's Evidence 74
    We Must Repent of all Our Evils................................75
    Repentance is What We Must Do, Ahead of Time 77
    The Reward of Iniquity or the Recompense of the Reward......78
    Withdraw or Withdrawals 80
    The Untouchables 81

Chapter 4: Repentance In the Book of Leviticus 83
    Carnal Knowledge is the Knowledge of Salvation 83
    The Head of the Bull is Cattle-Mindedness.....................87
    A Law Abiding Citizen..88
    Repentance is the Affliction of The Soul......................89
    The Law of Leprosy...90
    Leprous America..91
    Weapons of Mass Destruction 91

A Day to Atone and a Day of Salvation 92
To Appease the Gods 94
Fodder for the Gods 95
The Law of Repentance 96
To Please Almighty God..97
Our Atonement is Our Involvement....................................98
The "House of Replies" 99
A Cell Within a Box 100

Chapter 5: Repentance In the Book of Numbers 103
To Bear the Iniquity 103
The Smoking Gun/Relic 103
Leadership as a Barometer...105
Keep the Charge...106
A Now Word of Faith is not to be Repented of 107
Meat in God's House 108

Chapter 6: Repentance In the Book of Deuteronomy.....109
Repentance, Even in the Latter Days................................109
To Remain Impenitent is to Remain Ignorant of Our Future..110
Repentance Will Cause God to Rejoice Over Us for the Good...110
Carnality as Dung/Putting on the Dog.............................111
The Dung Smear 112
Carnality, the Land Mines of the Soul 113
Mind Your Own Business 114
A Shovel Among Your Weapons 115
God Does Not Want to Step in It 116
Times of War Should be Times of Reformation 117
Repentance as a Tool of the Trade 117
The Proverb of the Shovel 118
The Shovel Known as Repentance....................................118
The Reason and the Purpose..119
Before the Well, There was the Shovel..............................120

Chapter 7: Repentance In the Book of Joshua 121
- Impressions of Deception 121
- Finally, Somebody Caught the Revelation 122
- Something Sinister 123
- The A'chan Factor and the Accursed Thing 124

Chapter 8: Repentance In the Book of Judges 125
- To Judge is to Self Examine 125
- I Don't Know! 126
- A Crisis Intervention Technique 127

Chapter 9: Repentance In the Book of Ruth 129
- Origin of Incest 129
- Carnal Progeny 129
- The Caste System 130
- Repentance Given to the Gentiles 131
- A Method of Operation 132
- Progeny Means Fruit 133
- The Progeny of Repentance 133

Chapter 10: Repentance In the Book of 1st Samuel 135
- The Mantle of Repentance 135
- The Oil and the Wine 136
- The Iniquity of Stubbornness 137
- The "Yada, Yada, Yada," of "Yea But" 138
- Legal Claims 140
- Illustrated "Buts" 141

Chapter 11: Repentance In The Book of 2nd Samuel 145
- Repentance Must Cost Something 145
- Truth or Consequences 145
- Foolishness is Carnality 146
- The Catered Heart 147

Chapter 12: Repentance In The Book of 1st Kings 149
- In League with Our Lobbyist 149
- Presumption Negates Repentance 150

Chapter 13: Repentance In the Book of 2nd Kings 151
   Talk About Going to Hell in a Handbasket 151
   The Church that is Defined by Faith and Repentance 152
   The Line of Righteous Judgment 152
   Repentance Brings Restoration 153

BOOK 2: FREEDOM II
Chapter 14: Repentance In the Book of 1st Chronicles 3
   The Cities of Refuge 3
   Our Kinsman Redeemer 4
   The Altar as Asylum Vs the Altar of Asylum 4
   The Cities of Refuge were not Permanent Abodes 5
   From Carnality to Spiritual Maturity 6
   Jurisdiction 7
   The Skirts of the Vatican 7
   The Six Cities of Refuge 8
   A Circus Act 10
   The Clandestine Operation of Carnality 12

Chapter 15: Repentance In the Book of 2nd Chronicles 15
   Name Your Criteria 174 16
   A Lifestyle of Repentance is a Solemn Covenant with Almighty God 16
   Repentance is that which We Do for Others 17
   Repentance as a Rod of Correction 18
   Age Has Nothing to do with It, but Repentance Does 19

Chapter 16: Repentance In The Book of Ezra 21
   A Ready Scribe in the Land of Persia (Iraq/Iran) 21
   Appointed is Different from Chosen 22

Chapter 17: Repentance In The Book of Nehemiah 25
   A Man at the Right Place for the Right Time 26
   These Walls Had to be Maintained 27

Chapter 18: Repentance In The Book of Esther 29

    Intercourse in the Inner Court 29

Chapter 19: Repentance In the Book of Job 31
    The Abominations of Carnality 31
    Habeas Corpus is a Demand to Bring that Man to Court .. 31
    Making Amends for Carnality 32
    I Abhor Myself in Dust and Ashes 34

Chapter 20: Repentance In the Book of Psalms 37
    The Law of Repentance 37
    Opening Arguments: A Previously Documented
       Homicide Case 39
    The Charges of the Accused 42
    Trial Proceedings & Court Stipulations 45
    Stipulation 1: Specific Mercy for Specific Sin 45
    Stipulation 2: David Shouldered His Guilt and Shame ... 46
    The Ma' shak and the Ma' lach 47
    Conviction is a Useful Tool 48
    Circumstances Involved & the Ramifications It Caused 49
    Stipulation 3: Sin Victimizes God 49
    Stipulation 4: Carnality Must Be Acknowledged 50
    Stipulation 5: God is All Knowing 50
    A Psychological Profile 51
    The Four Quadrants of Self 53
    Stipulation 6: Honoring the Faith Contract 57
    Stipulation 7: Repentance Thwarts the Difficulties
       of Life 59
    Stipulation 8: Carnal Satisfaction or Spiritual
       Sanctification 60
    Stipulation 8a: A Case for Amnesty 62
    Stipulation 9: O God! Retool My Life 62
    Stipulation 9a: Quid Pro Quo 63
    R & R 64
    Stipulation 10: Which Cast Are You Talking About? 64
    Repentance That Should be Suspect 66
    Stipulation 11: The Freedom of a Liberated Heart 67

Stipulation 11a: Salvation's Nomenclature 67
Stipulation 12: The Defense of a Liberated Heart 69
Stipulation 13: Practical Instruction Begets Practical
  Faith 69
Stipulation 14: Blood Guiltiness 71
Salvation is Never to be Neglected 71
  Stipulation 14a: The Tongue of Righteousness 72
Stipulation 15: Repentance Must Never be Ignored
  or Neglected 74
  Stipulation 15a: Sacrifices of the Heart 74
  Stipulation 15b: Make a Joyful Noise 75
A Thorn in the Flesh 77
Closing Arguments: To Build the Spiritual Walls of
  Righteousness 78
Elements of the Law of Repentance 80

Chapter 21: Repentance in the Book of Proverbs 83
The First Principle of Repentance 83
Faith and Repentance Go Hand in Hand 84
The Difference Between an Argument and a Debate 85
What is Righteousness? 87
Scriptural Examples of the Righteousness of God 89
Righteousness Must be Sought After 91
Righteousness Must be Taught 92
The Influence of Righteousness 95
The Purpose of God's Righteousness 98
The Duplicity of Judgment 104
Three Natures 106
The Purpose and Reason of and for Righteousness 107
The Stampede of the Righteous 109
The Fruit of Righteousness 109
The Sacrifices of Righteousness 111
How does God Reveal His Righteousness? 112
The Standard of Righteousness is the Flag of Faith 114
The Insignia of Righteousness 116
The Guidon 117

Righteousness as a Drill Instructor 118
Hop-A-Long, Skip-A-Long Carnality 119

Chapter 22: Repentance In the Book of Ecclesiastes 121
It's All About Carnality! 121
No Righteous Judgment, No Execution............................122
Moved With Envy 123
The Subject of the Sons of Men 125
We Must Be Smarter than the Equipment 126
Carnal Bestiality 127
Man's Probation is a Time of Conformity to a Godly
  Moral Obligation 128
The Possibility of Conformity 130
Just What Are you Doing? 132
The Whole Duty of Man 134
That Which is Deep is Known by He Who is
  Deeper Still 135

Chapter 23: Repentance In the Book of Isaiah 137
Sin is a Voluntary Transgression of the Moral Law 137
What is Voluntariness? 139
Selfishness: The Deifying of Self 140
Come Now, Let Us Reason Together 141
The Condition of "If" 142
Woe is Me! I am Undone! 143
The Parasite of the Soul 144
The Kiln of Righteousness 144
The Furnace of Repentance 145
A Man of Unclean Lips 146
The Call in that Day 147
Carnality Shall Not be Purged Until the Day You Die 148
Flopping About on a Dry Dock 149
Double for Your Trouble 150
Wake Up Thou Sluggard! 151
A Bargain with Death 151
A Day of Trouble and the Day of Salvation 152

Baring It All Means to Come Clean 153
Ghost Towns, Abandoned Buildings and Waste Land 154
Wicked Ways and Premeditated, Unrighteous Thoughts ..155
Ulterior Motives of Predetermined, Carnal Mind Sets 156
The Stuff of Fairy Tales 158
The Book of Rebellion 158

Chapter 24: Repentance In the Book of Jeremiah 163
The Face of an Effeminate Man 163
A Method of Application 165
Solomon's Chariot 165
Playing the Harlot with Many Lovers 167
Self Exaltation 168
The Topography of Man's Carnality 169
Who Are You in League With? 170
Petra: A Physical Parallel of a Spiritual Truth 171
From a Prison to a Prism 172
Self Absorbed in Their Own Self Centeredness 175
There is No Shame! 176
Religious Overtones and Sanctimonious Mind Sets 176
A Strong Indictment to the Ungodly for Righteousness ...177
Coddled and Justified Carnality 180
Birds of Ill Omen 181
That Thou Mayest be Saved 182
The Copulation of Carnality 183
God Alone Reserves the Right to Reverse 184
The Heart of the Matter is Man's Character 185
Infidelity is Apostasy 186
What is Apostasy? 187
The Dry, Hot Wind of Judgment 188
His Horses are Swifter than Eagles 190
The Travail of the Soul 192
Till the Fallow Ground 193
Getting Bloody in the Spirit 194
An Imperfection to the Vessel 195
The Finger Prints of Carnality 196

Self Torment is to Be a Terror to Thy Carnal Self
and to Thy Carnal Friends 198
God's Promises are not Different from His Commands ...199
Amend Your Ways 200

Chapter 25: Repentance In The Book of Lamentations 203
That Which Is Better 203
How Could This Happen? 204
What is Selfishness? 206
The School of Selfishness 206
Characteristics of Selfishness 208
A National Funeral 209
The Birthing of Righteous Judgment 210
Substance Must Precede Evidence 211
The Measure of Faith and the Measuring Line
of Judgment 212

Chapter 26: Repentance In the Book of Ezekiel 215
Weapons of Judgment 216
The Pen is Mightier than the Sword 217
Every Tongue that Shall Rise Against Thee in Judgment ...218
To Judge Means to Endure 219
Wickedness in the Sanctuary 222
A Mitigation of Judgment 223
Repent and Turn Away From Your Idols 224
Carnality Shall Be Our Ruin 225
Errant Proverbs 226
The Difference Between a Confession and a Profession 227
A Man's Lifestyle and His Name Are Equally The Same ...228
Observations Are Not Judgment Calls 229
Repentance is Essential to Purity and Righteousness 230
The Death of the Saints 232
The Wickedness of the Wicked 233
The Way of the Lord is not Equal 234

List of Axioms: Truths of Repentance 237

Addendum: The Utility and Application of Repentance:...... 265

BOOK 3: FREEDOM III
Chapter 27: Repentance In the Book of Daniel 3
- The Unencumbered Soul 3
- Show The Reality of Your Repentance 4
- Animal Impulses and Carnal Tendencies 5
- Liberate Yourself From Your Iniquitous Thoughts 7
- Man's Carnality is the Scent Which the Dogs of Hell Follow ...7
- The Dogs of Hell 8

Chapter 28: Repentance In the Book of Hosea 11
- The Very First 11
- Spiritual Adultery 12
- The Progenitive Qualities of Repentance 14
- A Journey to Self Recovery 15
- To Judge Yourself Unworthy of Eternal Life 17
- The Golden Rule of Obligation 20

Chapter 29: Repentance In the Book of Joel 25
- The Rules of Engagement Have Changed 25
- Awake to Repentance 27
- Rend Your Heart and not Your "holy" Garments 28
- Torn "holy" Garments 29
- Cross Dressers and Switch Hitters Are an Abomination 32
- Shearing Stress of Carnality 33
- Another Man's Scruples 36
- Binding and Loosing 38
- Create a Faith Environment for God to Move 39

Chapter 30: Repentance In the Book of Amos 41
- Establish Judgments at the Gates 41
- Repentance Postpones God's Judgment 43
- To Seek Means to Activate Litigation 44
- Navy S.E.A.L. (Sea, Air and Land) 45
- The Treader of Grapes and the Winepress of God 47

Portraits of Travail 49
The Identity of the Seal 50
Repentance as a "Stay of Execution 51
Final Appeals for a "Stay of Execution 52
Only Those on Death Row Know 53
Prisonization and Institutionalization 53
The Absence of Righteous Judgment 54
Workers of Righteousness 55

Chapter 31: Repentance In the Book of Obediah 57
Just Who Was Esau, Anyway? 57
An Underlying Current 58
A Lifestyle of Carnality 59
What's in Your Wallet? 60
Respect Your Inheritance 61
The Elder to Serve the Younger 61
A Savior to Judge 61

Chapter 32: Repentance In the Book of Jonah 63
The Pursuit is On 63
The Hazards of a Pursuit 64
A Whale of a Time 64
This Fish Represents Bondage and Bondage has Depth 65
The Roots of the Mountains 67
Three Types of Mountains 68
Mountain of Righteousness to Arise Above the
   Mountains of Carnality 76
The Rejection of Bondage 77
Blood Boiling Mad 78
We Must Guard Ourselves Against the Gourds of Life 79

Chapter 33: Repentance In the Book of Micah 83
The First to be Punished 83
Make Thee Bald 84
Balderdash 85
The Balderdash of Repentance 85

Chapter 34: Repentance In The Book of Nahum 87
An Antecedent to Destruction 87

Chapter 35: Repentance in the Book of Habakkuk 91
A Tale of Two Cities 91
America's Ground Zero 91
That Which Begs the Question 92
America's Wake Up Call 93
Judgment and Righteousness, Ignored 93
Saviors of God 94
The Exalted State of Carnality 94

Chapter 36: Repentance In the Book of Zephaniah 97
A Time For Repentance 97
The Cycle of Grace 99

Chapter 37: Repentance In the Book of Haggai 101
The Lollygagging Church 101
The Dawdling Church 102
Carnal Bruising 103
Not Yet! 104
Consider Your Ways 104
Broken Spokes 105

Chapter 38: Repentance In the Book of Zechariah 107
From a Tradition to a Transition 107
Ishmael verses Isaac 108
Desert Storm 109

Chapter 39: Repentance In the Book of Malachi 111
The Burden of the Word is Repentance 111
Pangs of Death 112
From a Reproof to a Reproach 112
The Skill of Debate 115
Objection #1: In What Way Have You Loved Us? 115
Objection #2: How and in What Way Have We Despised
Your Name? 117

Objection #3: Since There is no Profit in It, Why Bother?....117
Objection #4: A Polluted Altar 118
Objection #5: What a Drudgery and Weariness This is! 118
Objection #6: Why Does He reject Our Offerings? 119
Objection #7: In What Way Have We Wearied Him? 119
Objection #8: How Shall We Return? 120
Objection #9: In What Way Have We Robbed you? 121
Answer a Question With a Question 122

Chapter 40: The Seven Furnaces of Mystery Babylon 125
Case Law: To Establish a Precedent as a Basis for an Argument 127
Furnace #1: Fear to be Replaced by Faith [trust] 129
Careful! Don't Get Incinerated 129
Furnace #2: The Furnace of Repentance & Sanctification 133
Getting Bloody in the Spirit 133
Blazing Your Own Trail 134
Furnace #3: Furnace of Forensic Cross-Examination 136
The Trial of One's Heart 136
Furnace #4: Increase Your Property Value 137
Furnace #5: The Righteous Judgment of the Church 139
Overcoming One's Hardness of Carnality 139
Gold of Faith and the Silver of Carnality 141
Furnace #6: The Furnace of Righteous Litigation 143
Flies Are Drawn to Uncovered Food 143
We Must Be Taught the Proper, Safe Use of Fire 144
A Rolled Newspaper 145
Furnace #7: The Wrath of God's Righteous Judgment 146
Carnality to Burn 146
Yellow is to Brass as Gold is to Faith 147
Closing Comments 148

List of Axioms: Truths of Repentance 149
Addendum: The Utility and Application of Repentance: 189

Author's Preface

If you are anything like me, then you will appreciate provocative, spiritual insights which challenge established theological dogmas. For so many years, I have often mused over the many theological concepts of Bible doctrine. And through these years, I have asked spiritual leadership, church members and the "man on the street" to provide for me an acceptable explanation for such doctrines as faith, repentance, grace, righteousness, sanctification, consecration, etc. only to be given a vague, shallow answer from each individual and for each subject. In other words, they failed to provide me something fresh and new. Their answers parroted that which I already knew or have previously heard. To a great extent, I learned, through this census, that the truth of the gospel has been hidden under a false, philosophical pretense. Consequently, these answers only confirmed my heart felt witness of this reality.

The responses I received convinced me of three basic societal mind sets, which seemingly reflected a social conscience of illiteracy in varying degrees of biblical truth. To wit, it's common knowledge that the national illiteracy rate verges on thirty percent, and there are some counties within certain states where the illiteracy rate is even higher! For instance, it's been said that the illiteracy rate in Okmulgee County in Oklahoma is thirty-eight percent! If this is the case, then it is reasonable to suspect that such illiteracy would also bleed over and into the comprehension of scriptural truth. And given the worldly condition of the church en-masse today, I can understand why this is so.

As to faith, the answers provided by church leadership were the basic responses such as, *"So then faith comes by hearing and hearing the word of God." (Rom. 10:17)* or *"Now faith is the sub-*

stance of things hoped for and is the evidence of things not seen." (Heb. 11:1) As to repentance, the best I have heard was simply turning around or turning your back on sin. Secondly, the church goer would refer to these basic Scriptures, but without a proper recitation of them, or they were uncertain of the scripture references themselves! Thirdly, the "man on the street," had his own vague, philosophical assumption as did a good majority of church folk! After all, as any church is a cross section of the community in which it is located, the parishioners are the very same people who come from that society.

I ask the reader to remember that this work is a personal revelation to me and that I do not claim to possess the final, definitive word on the theological subjects contained herein. Having stated this however, I do maintain that due to this extensive investigation of and about the many aspects and truths of a lifestyle of repentance, I do know far more about repentance than I have ever known or ever considered before.

This investigation, in the light of Scripture, contains the revelation of a Lifestyle of Repentance which embraces consecration, holiness, sanctification, righteousness, and godliness. You will find that this investigation is not an easy read, but it is hard hitting, strong and very provocative, and as you read through, your mind will be forced to consider new perspectives and concepts.

As you will learn, repentance presupposes carnality just as iniquity presupposes carnality. By presuppose, I mean too say that since iniquity is indigenous within the soul of each and every man, Almighty God's remedy for this carnal tragedy, is His gift of repentance to fallen humanity. He has granted repentance to mankind so that impenitent men would acknowledge their iniquity aka lie-based-thinking thereby, exposing and identifying this contamination, as an element of sin, within their souls. As pertaining to carnality, suffice it too say that this investigation contains carnal knowledge, a Roman Catholic expression, which simply refers to the knowledge of carnality. Moreover, repentance presupposes carnality just as revival presupposes a backsliding church. This then makes repentance a command of scripture for it is also the doctrine of God and as such, it is the knowledge of salvation. And I might add, that this knowledge of salvation will lead you to understand the duplicity of judgment as being for the salvation of the soul but against the iniquitous thoughts and the carnality within the soul.

Within these pages, you will find specific Truths of Repentance which are sequentially numbered. Each truth pertains to the matter of content and are revelations of and about repentance and the related attributes of it, such as godliness, righteousness, etc. As you absorb these Truths of Repentance you will experience personal transitions from the generally accepted doctrinal or theological traditions. In doing so, the scriptural knowledge that you once dismissed, shall become the scriptural knowledge you would now embrace! It is further noted, that as you digest this investigation, you will salt your soul with the word of God's righteousness as you assault your carnality. Consequently, your soul will be silently and secretly "cured" as you marinade your heart with God's anointed Word, which is His instructions in righteousness!

Let me conclude this by saying that the style of content and the flow of continuity which this investigation possesses, was written with a law enforcement officer's philosophical view point of jurisprudence, but from the standpoint of a prisoner. Therefore, it may be understood that the revelations of and about a lifestyle of repentance are substantiated with numerous truths that are true to Scripture, true to reason and true to life so that repentance would become to you, one over whelming and harmonious revelation.

Whereas, any prisoner becomes acquainted with the regimen of the correctional facility of which he is a resident, likewise you, the reader, shall also acquaint yourself with God's Incarceration Instructions for repentance is a lifestyle to live as a prisoner of Jesus Christ. Again, the investigative mind set, which any law enforcement officer possesses, shall be evident to you and having said this, you shall also recognize that the central theme of repentance has been written from the perspective of a prisoner.

This investigation contains many associations and metaphors common to life's encounters. Such similies will help clarify the truths which logic mandates must be demonstrated. As you progress through this work, you will find that your existing, entrenched philosophical opinions and other theological postulations will be challenged and hopefully brought to a logical consequence or outcome. Your emotions will be stirred, and it's my prayer for you that your conduct and your behavior will be changed as your carnality is suppressed.

I therefore, commend this work to you the reader, and to the corporate Body of Christ. It is my intent that you experience a sudden impact of such proportions that you will literally buckle at the knees! It is my intent also that your soul would be penetrated by the large caliber projectiles of divine revelation, so much so, that your soul would be perforated with the light of God's truth! I congratulate you dear reader, for having the courage to embark on a journey of the renewal of your mind and for a changed character.

As my brief census revealed, there are three classes of societal mind sets. Therefore, it is reasonable to assume that there are also three levels or conditions of mental acuity as the following will attest.

1. Idle minds are preoccupied with self, the material thing and others.

2. Average minds are preoccupied with situations, circumstances and events.

3. Great minds are preoccupied with concepts, ideas, and a

pursuit of knowledge and other disciplines of thought.

"The mind once expanded can never return to its original dimensions." Oliver Wendell Holmes

On a more personal note, I am an ordained minister who is also a retired California Highway Patrol Officer. I served the Golden State twelve years during which time Almighty God allowed me the distinct pleasure of ministry to the public. My style of writing, which is an economy of words, has come about due to the required disciplines of report writing, which law enforcement demands.

FREEDOM III - Carnality, Denial and the Judgments of God

Introduction

The Reason and the Purpose for Repentance

Romans 2:4-5
Or do you think lightly of the riches of His kindness and tolerance and patience, not knowing that the kindness of God leads you to repentance? But because of your stubbornness and unrepentant heart you are storing up wrath for yourself in the day of wrath and revelation of the righteous judgment of God,...

Romans 11:32
For God has imprisoned everyone in disobedience so he could have mercy on everyone.

As I read *Romans 11:32* in my NLT version, I was captured by verse 32 specifically. The word *'imprisoned.'* Else where in scripture, Paul states that he was a *prisoner* of Jesus Christ. Even in the book of Phileon, Paul stated this about himself again. As I pondered verse 32, and I compared *Romans 2:4*, I noticed a *reason* and a *purpose*. In other words, by reason of my imprisonment, the PURPOSE for *repentance* is presented. Because humanity is imprisoned in the cell block of his disobedience, he becomes *pent up* in his carnal mindedness and as such, his carnal mind evinces the existence of his iniquitous thoughts (aka: Lie Based Thinking). With this said, it is important that humanity (you and me included) acquire specific working knowledge about our manner of thinking, capturing each thought and bringing each thought into obedience. *(cf. 2 Cor.10:5)* As we do so, we will gain a better understanding of *carnal knowledge* for without this, each person will simply deny that they are carnal solely based upon ignorance. In doing so your identification in Jesus will be established, for you see dear friend, repentance has nothing to do with the confession of your sin but it has everything to do with your identification with God through His Son Jesus Christ.

With all this said, as an analogy consider that as we cultivate a lifestyle of repentance within we are complying with God's *incarceration instructions*! Even in the "lock up" each inmate must learn and comply with the institution's incarceration instructions. If the inmate does comply, the time served will go easier and in time his *freedom* will be experienced. IF the inmate chooses to disobey these Instructions, then the time served will be arduous, complicated extending his imprisonment. And when you consider life in the *penitentiary*, the inmate lives day after day in a structured routine of limitations and restrictions deemed necessary towards the renewing of his mind and heart in hopes that the inmate would finally become an asset to himself and to society.

For the inmate/prisoner, the forced lifestyle of repentance was 24/7 throughout the days of his internment. The prisoner lived it, breathed it, ate it, wore it. slept in it and endured it throughout the days of his living behind bars. For this prisoner, it was the atmosphere, of life. It is inhaling and exhaling the air of penitence; drinking in the reason and the purpose for his jail time experience. So for the rest of humanity, take this analogy of a prisoner's lock up and apply the spiritual truth and concept to your life so that you may cultivate a deeper relationship with Jesus Christ.

Chapter 27
Repentance in the Book of Daniel

The Unencumbered Soul

Daniel, Shadrach, Meshach and Abednego were determined to maintain their meatless diet. *(cf. Dan. 1:8-17)* The result being, that they were plumper and their countenance did glow all the more than the other youths taken into Babylonian captivity along with them. But why did Daniel and his friends abstain from the king's meats? It is common knowledge, that we are what we eat. Many of the physical maladies which are so prevalent to humanity, are the direct result of consuming inappropriate foods or addictive substances. Although Daniel and his three friends might have been aware of this fact, I believe that the actual reason as too why they abstained from meats was their own conviction towards the Lord their God. *(cf. Rom. 14:20-22)* As a benefit, their souls remained undefiled and their brains were unencumbered with contagions or other toxins, enabling them to excel in their required Chaldean studies and with their pursuit of wisdom.

Nowadays, dietary supplements are available to stimulate a person's cognitive processes so that their declarative, short term memory would be provoked. This intimates a spiritual parallel correlating foods and other substances ingested physically, with the consumption of God's Word of faith and His righteousness digested spiritually. **Truth #188: Whereas, anything consumed or ingested may either defile or enhance one's anatomy, like-**

wise that which is sensually assimilated may also pollute or cleanse the soul by arousing carnality or spirituality, for the kingdom of God is not in food or drink only, but it is righteousness, peace and joy in the Holy Ghost! *(cf. Rom. 14:17; Lk. 17:20-21)*

The parallels are to obvious. What we eat beyond a basic need, has a direct effect on self indulgence. **Truth #189: Through a lifestyle of repentance, the soul remains undefiled and the saint stays reconciled to God!** Thoughts, what the mind consumes in self gratification, is directly stored as carnal fat cells which contaminate the soul. The burdened soul therefore loses its ability to remain reconciled to God, or it is distracted from the things of God because of the resurgence of iniquitous thoughts!

Show the Reality of Your Repentance

Daniel 4:24-33 AMP

"...[you] ***break off*** *your sins and* ***show the reality of your repentance*** *by righteousness (right standing with God and moral and spiritual rectitude and rightness in every area and relation) and* ***liberate yourself from your iniquities by showing*** *mercy and loving kindness to the poor and the oppressed, that if the king will* ***repent*** *there may be possibly a continuance and lengthening of your peace and tranquility and a healing of* ***your error.****"* (emphasis mine)

These passages refer to the startling metamorphosis of King Nebuchadnezzar when his physical body was transformed into a beast of the field. Like King Solomon whose vanity and pursuit of the earthly thing caused him to acknowledge, that without the wisdom of God, life is not worth living; Nebuchadnezzar would also acknowledge this same truth. Whereas, Solomon was beastly in his carnality, Nebuchadnezzar became the beast of the field as a direct testimonial of his carnality! **Truth #190:**

The reality of repentance provides longevity of life as it prevails over man's carnality, because repentance keeps the beast in its cage! Talk is cheap! The point of these verses stresses the intent that repentance must be demonstrated. It's more than the response to the evangelistic altar call for conversion or salvation! It's more than just turning from your sin. Repentance is a lifestyle which must be demonstrated, for it qualifies faith!

Animal Impulses and Carnal Tendencies

Ecclesiastes 3:18 AMP

"I said in my heart regarding the subject of the sons of men, God is trying (separating and sifting) them, that they may see that by themselves [under the sun without God] they are but like the beasts."

Colossians 3:5-6 AMP

*"So kill (deaden, deprive of power) the evil desire lurking in your members [**those animal impulses** and all that is earthly in you that is employed in sin]: sexual vice, impurity, sensual appetites, unholy desires, and all greed and covetousness, for that is idolatry (the defying of self and other created things of God). It is on account of these [very sins] that the [holy] anger of God is ever coming upon the sons of disobedience (those who are obstinately opposed to the divine will)."* (emphasis mine)

Whether sinner or saint, as long as a man physically lives, he shall possess iniquity all the days of his life. *(cf. Is. 22:14)* This truth then validates that the carnal mind is the mind of the unregenerate soul. Therefore, the carnality of an unregenerate soul is the substance of a constitutionally flawed character, because within every soul there exists strongholds and imaginations which are lodged in the carnal mind, which is the mind of the unregenerate soul. For example, strongholds are the active result of vain imaginations lodged within the mind. The existence of these strongholds tends to produce impressions of imprisonment, entombment or bondage. Likewise, vain imaginations are the foolish concepts, arguments, piecemeal theology or other misrepresentations of Scripture or religious dogmas that are contrary to God's Word. **Truth #191: Through a lifestyle of repentance, the saint suppresses his carnality as he purifies his mind of iniquitous thoughts!** The Church must remember that Satan schemes according to the saints ignorance and misunderstanding of scriptural truth.

The word *carnal* for instance, means, "pertaining to the flesh, to be animalistic, unregenerate 1. Flesh as a strip of skin; meat of an animal. 2. Human nature [physical and moral] passions, appetites, affections, cravings lust." (Strong's Exhaustive Concordance) Furthermore, the Roger's Thesaurus, reference #1029.16 defines carnal to be; "worldly, earthly, terrestrial, mundane, temporal, unspiritual, profane, carnal, secular, worldly minded, earthly minded, carnal minded, materialistic." Actually, reference #1029, items 1-22 all relate to the carnality of human nature.

Consider for a moment the three basic impulses of any animal. They are:
- 1. To propagate its species,
- 2. Survival,
- 3. Creature comforts.

Now compare the carnal tendencies of a carnal mind, belonging to an unregenerate person. Without righteousness, any person will also possess these same animalistic traits and even then some! Have you ever thought that there are things animals just won't do? But what do we continually observe about the fallen carnal [sinful] condition of man? Our newspapers are filled with:
- 1. Sexual vice, impurity and sensual appetites,
- 2. Preoccupation with survival with such platitudes as: dog

eat dog, jungle rules, rat race, and the survival of the fittest.
- 3. Creature comforts such as materialism, love of money, covetousness, greed and the like.
- 4. Beheadings, mass genocide, governmental and religious oppression. Not once do we read that some animal had committed these crimes against society! *(cf. Col. 3:5-6; Gal. 5:19-21; Rev. 21:8)*

Liberate Yourself from Iniquitous Thoughts

In Daniel 4:24-33, Almighty God provides for the saint a way of escape out of temptation and self torment. Daniel said to Nebuchadnezzar that he could liberate himself from his iniquities, by showing mercy and loving kindness and that if he did so, there would be perhaps a continuation of his reign and a lengthening of the peace and tranquility of his kingdom. The fact that Daniel said this speaks of the grace which the Lord God had for Nebuchadnezzar. It is evident therefore, that God did not want to destroy the king, but that the king would come to repentance and live uprightly before God. Had Nebuchadnezzar repented, this method of escape would have prolonged the time and the distance he would have continued to remain free to rule and reign. We saw this with King Hezekiah, when the Lord God extended his life fifteen more years. *(cf. Is. 38:-5)*

Man's Carnality is the Scent
Which the Dogs of Hell Follow After

A well thought out plan could be successful for the inmate who is determined to break out. Even though this fugitive would be temporarily free, he could not escape the self torment of his iniquitous thoughts. He would be tormented by the fact that he is an escapee and that it would be just a matter of time before he is either caught or killed in his escapade. The estrangement between he and society would be so obvious that his alienation from a former, civil life would be as a large neon sign flashing "FUGITIVE" before him, for the duration of his evasion. Adrenalin would circulate throughout his body, because he would be in the fight or flight mode. His desperation would excite this anatomical response within him to the circumstance. He would be a raging bull, who has no regard for property or person. His selfishness would be in full swing as he evades the authorities. **The dogs of hell would soon be in hot pursuit of him, because his carnality is the scent which they follow after.** Why should anyone want to pursue a life like this? And yet most do, when they are running form God. Almighty God asks the question, Why should the wicked die in their sin?

The Dogs of Hell

The fugitive continues to flee. He becomes skillful in his evasion, making up fictitious names and picking up other erroneous identification. He finds himself in violation of identity theft, often taking on names of those already deceased or altering his own physical appearance, all the while trying to avoid the dogs of hell that are constantly hounding his conscience and gnawing at his heels. What are these dogs of hell? They are the demons of self torment and iniquitous thoughts of a guilty, carnal mind *(Mens Rea)! The fact that the police dog assists the officer in the performance of his duty, validates the fact that when a man is in his carnality, he has become his own best friend or in this case, his worst enemy!* After all, it takes a dog to hunt a dog. Recently, a young woman was convicted of murder in the state of Texas. Her case was high profile due to the extenuating circumstances involved in the case. During her trial, she testified of her remorse and courageously accepted her sentence, even to the point of stating that she was deserving of it. In essence, she said that she was relieved when she was finally arrested, because she had trouble living with herself. Her testimony proved once again that the dogs of hell had successfully done their job. But from where do these dogs come? Do these carnal K-9s exist within carnal man, or are they released by another entity to track and then hunt down their intended victim or prey? Scriptures provide the answer to this pet question.

Revelations 22:15
"For without are dogs, and sorcerers, and whoremongers, and murderers, and idolaters, and whosoever loveth and maketh lies."

Psalms 22:16
"For dogs have compassed me: the assembly of the wicked have enclosed me: they pierced my hands and my feet."

Psalms 68:23
"That thy foot may be dipped in the blood of thine enemies, and the tongue of thy dogs in the same."

Phillippians 3:2 AMP
"Beware of dogs, beware of evil doers, beware of concision [cutting down, mutilation]."

So from these few verses, it is apparent that a carnal man is that dog. This therefore intimates that the dogs of hell exists within him. The fact that any dog is carnivorous, in that it is a meat eater, suggests that the mutilation caused by carnal men shows the reality of the dogs of hell. And just as any dog would be a pet, also suggests that carnal man has made a darling of his carnality! Therefore dear saint, beware of the carnal dogs of hell! **Truth #192: Whereas, any pet should be trained to obey, likewise carnal man must also attend obedience school to suppress his carnal tendencies. He does so through a lifestyle of**

repentance, which is his obedience to the instructions in righteousness! *(cf. 2 Tim. 3:16)*

To wit, what denominationalism is to man's institution and tradition, secularism is to a godless, worldly church! The established, dysfunctional church has failed miserably in its mission to convert this sinful world, even to disciple the congregations in accordance to Scripture! *It is the witness of my heart, that church leadership has opted to take the path of least resistance, which is to return to or remain in the familiar domain of denominationalism or their tradition.* In doing so, the full counsel of God is ignored and is avoided altogether. Specifically, that the preaching of the cross, as it pertains to sanctification, has been for the most part disregarded and replaced with a carnal gospel of avarice [greed]. The result being, mega-churches have sprung up like weeds in the vineyard of humanity! Their congregations are malnourished and the people remain unsanctified. Because carnality is denied and righteousness remains aloof, so many in these churches, have no concept of repentance, since it is no longer communicated from the pulpits, as a corresponding action which validates faith!

Chapter 28
Repentance in the Book of Hosea

The Very First

Have you ever gone through a season in your life when you experienced firsts? These first events were life changing situations either for the better or for the worst, weren't they? Either way, they were to you a first. In fact, life itself is filled with all kinds or aspects of firsts, isn't it? For example, I was first born on a specific date and at a specific time. I first went to school and then I first graduated from school. Where upon I first enlisted and was honorably discharged. I first was employed as a law enforcement officer and I experienced my first retirement. I authored my first book and have first resided in Texas, where I first attended and graduated from Bible College. I then relocated to Oklahoma, which was another first. etc. In each and every event, my life has been altered and the lives of others around me have been effected. The Prophet Hosea was the very first to prophecy righteous judgment against Israel. (cf. Matthew Henry's Commentary overview, col. 2, para. 2, page 1462) And because he was the first to preach repentance, and write and then publish these divine prophecies, the other prophets did borrow his specific prophetic utterances in their prophecies about or against Israel of their day as well. Prophets were tutors of carnality to the people of God and so are all faithful ministers today, who courageously preach salvation of the soul from the vestiges of iniquity. I find it interesting that Hosea did not have the option to coddle the people to his prophecies. He spoke them cold turkey, point blank and from the *git-go! This abrupt and blunt approach seemingly would become the manner of all of God's prophets in their delivery, because it was a necessary exhortation with strong urging and warning!* Through these prophets, Almighty God hammered it home, that the land was polluted because of the whoredom of the people! Prophets Isaiah, Jeremiah and Ezekiel also prophesied to the people of their wickedness, borrowing specific adages from Hosea in their discourses. For example: *Isaiah 31:8-9* and *37:36* speak of *Hosea 1:7. Jeremiah 7:34; 16:9; 25;10; Ezekiel 26:13* speak the same as *Hosea 2:11. Ezekiel 16:16* is taken from *Hosea 2:8.* Therefore one prophet confirms and corroborates another and all these worketh that one and self-same Spirit. (Matthew Henry's Commentary and introduction, column 2, item II, page 1462)

Spiritual Adultery

Hosea 1:2 AMP
"When the Lord first spoke with and through Hosea, the Lord said to him, Go, take to yourself a wife of harlotry and have children of her harlotry, for the land commits great whoredom by departing from the Lord."

Hosea 2:2b AMP
"...that she put away her [marks of] harlotry from her face and her adulteries from between her breasts."

With the aforementioned in mind, it is apparent then, that the Lord God had to alert the impenitent people of their whoredom. And because their carnality pertained to the spiritual, Almighty God employed His spiritual truth of language and interpretation. He commanded Hosea to marry a whore, and then to have children by her as a physical portrayal of their spiritual sin of adultery. So Hosea married a prostitute named Gomer and she bare three children, a son whose name was Jezreel (God-sows), and a daughter whose name was Lo-Ruhamah (Not pitied), and another son whose name was Lo-Ammi (Not my people). *(cf. Hos. 1:3-9)*

Spiritual adultery is apostasy from God and the things of God! *Apostasy* is defined, *"as the abandonment of what one has believed in as a faith, cause or principle and replacing it with another."* (Webster's) This then makes the proponent a renegade and is therefore guilty of being an apostate! Contextually, spiritual adultery is related to idolatry. No doubt that the stigma which Hosea obtained, as a result of this union with a harlot, and the prejudice which his family experienced, was a burdensome reproach to he and his family, because his union to Gomer was a paradigm [standard] to the sin of the people corporately. It was intended by God that the scorn which Hosea received from others, was such that their disgust with his marriage was a reflection of their own whoredom. Though his kids were born in wedlock, yet they still were children of whoredoms, because their mother was first a harlot. She was not a harlot due to an extramarital affair; but she was a whore from the beginning. Her marks [painted face] of harlotry upon her, represented the mark of a whore upon the foreheads of a harlot nation! *(cf. Jer. 3:1-3)* The fact that Gomer was a harlot first, before she became a mother justifies the title of Mother of Harlots. This intimates that those who were idolatrous then, were also children of whoredoms, and this made them all whoremongers! No telling how many children Gomer might have had out of wedlock, prior to her marriage to Hosea.

Jeremiah 3:14
"Turn O backsliding children, saith the Lord; for I am married unto to you..."

The people were charged with spiritual adultery [idolatry]. For a nation or a person to give that glory, which is due Almighty God, to the created thing and not to the Creator is idolatry and therefore spiritual adultery. The fact that Hosea did wed a whore suggests that the people of God had divorced themselves from God, due to their life of adultery, just as an unfaithful spouse would do in an extramarital affair. The text verses above, points out that God's people had embraced their whoredoms and suckled their carnality. This is indicated with the reference of the adulteries between their breasts in verse 2:2. **Truth #193: Spiritual adultery is the diametric condition to righteousness and is therefore a lifestyle of carnality, which embraces idolatry and suckles that which is morally depraved!** Those who practice spiritual adultery have banned themselves together as in an outlaw, renegade company. And as the Word of God states, no whoremonger shall enter the kingdom of God!

Revelations 22:14-15
"Blessed are they that do His commandments, that they may have right to the tree of life, and may enter in through the gates of the city. For without are dogs, and sorcerers, and whoremongers, and murderers, and idolaters, and whosoever that loveth and maketh a lie."

Progenitive Qualities of Repentance
Hosea 2:1-2 AMP
"Hosea, say to your brethren, Ammi [or You-are-My-people], and to your sisters, Ruhamah [or You-have-been-pitied-and-have-obtained-mercy]. Plead with your mother [your nation]; plead, for she is not My wife and I am not her Husband; plead, that she would put away her marks of harlotry from her face and her adulteries from between her breasts."

Through the grace of God, the progenitive qualities of repentance produces spiritual offspring. Specifically, as sons of God through the Spirit of Adoption which produces son ship. Presently, creation is expectantly waiting and longs for God's sons to be made known. And I might add, this does not mean too say that every church goer is a son of God! However, those saints of God who have adopted a lifestyle of repentance are, because they have qualified their faith! *(cf. Rom. 8:15-20)* **Truth #194: Through a lifestyle of repentance, the saint impregnates his soul with the richness that is of God, through faith in Christ alone, thereby propagating his salvation as a son of God!**

A Journey to Self Recovery

Hosea 14:1 AMP
"O Israel, return to the Lord your God, for you have stumbled and fallen [visited by calamity] due to your iniquity [carnality]."

Every saint is a potential candidate for a revival! Revival then, is a hunger and a thirst for change from carnal tendencies and self indulgent living, to godliness. *Whenever, a saint seeks after righteousness, everything about him is subject to change. For some, change is a first and the gift of repentance is the provision of grace which God has given to His Church, to facilitate this change. This makes self recovery a personal endeavor from carnality to righteousness.* Revival then, is a life changing experience whenever the saint allows himself to be recovered, because revival must be predicated by his hearts desire for it! *(cf. Dan. 4:24-33)*

Revival is established in faith and repentance. To recover yourself is to stir up the revival fire within your heart, because recovery is a thing to do. *Just as a Peace Officer would recover a stolen vehicle, a revival experience causes you to recover all that Satan has stolen, because you are that stolen property! What a pursuit of a thief is to law enforcement, the chase for righteousness is to the recovery of one's self from the clutches of carnality, because it is the personal activity of a godly pursuit which demands your involvement! This then makes your personal revival the flow of that which has been revived!*

>2 Timothy 2:25-26
>"In meekness instructing those who oppose themselves: if God peradventure **will give them repentance** to the acknowledging of the truth; and that they may **recover** themselves out of the snare of the devil, who are taken captive by him at his will." (emphasis mine)

Scripture teaches that the saints of God are not to be conformed to the things of this world, but that they are to be transformed [renewed, revived]. *(cf. Rom. 12:2)* This nonconformity denotes a radical change from carnality to righteousness. I've heard it said, *the opposite of courage is not cowardice or fear, but its opposite is conformity.* Scripture commands that the saints of God are not to be conformed to the patterns and methodologies of this wicked world. Therefore, this makes revival the opposite of religious and secular congruity and the transformation from a lifestyle of carnality to a lifestyle of repentance!

In the book of Acts, Paul and Barnabas were confronted by the religious Jews, who were offended by the conversions of the multitudes at the preaching of the gospel. These elitist Jews, as Scripture shows, profaned, contradicted, ridiculed and blasphemed every word that was preached. Finally, Paul and Barnabas spoke out boldly against these slanderous folk and said in essence, that it was necessary that God's message concerning salvation through Christ be preached to you first. But since you repudiate it, then you have judged yourselves unworthy of eternal life. *(cf. Acts 13:44-46)*

To Judge Yourself Unworthy of Eternal Life
Luke 9:22 AMP

*"Saying, The Son of Man must suffer many things and be [deliberately] disapproved and **repudiated** and rejected on the part of the elders and the chief priests and scribes, and be put to death and on the third day be raised [again]." (emphasis mine)*

Repudiate. Now here is a word worth looking into. Webster's Dictionary defines it to mean, "to put away, divorce, separation, to feel shame.
- 1. to refuse to have anything to do with; disown or cast off publicly
- 2. to refuse to accept or support, deny the truth of (a charge)
- 3. to refuse to acknowledge or pay a debt or an obligation."

Several key words are of significance pertaining to repentance and carnality.

▶ 1. *to put away.* The thought that comes to mind here is the death contract a mob would place against an intended victim. Such expressions as "waste him, eliminate him or deep six him" come to my mind. No matter how you may choose to regard it, the intention of these elitist Jews was to put away that which was preached, but also to put Paul and Barnabas away also. **Truth #195: Without a lifestyle of repentance, we waste ourselves, because we sentence ourselves to eternal death!**

▶ 2. *to divorce.* As stated earlier, any divorce must first be contemplated. This premeditation may take years, even decades, before it is finally materialized in a courtroom. These infidel Jews had already predetermined for themselves that they were unworthy of salvation and therefore, possessed ulterior motives as to why they slandered the gospel preached by Paul and Barnabas. Their blackened heart became evident to every body around, in that these obstinate Jews had manifested their true intent through their conduct and behavior, during this confrontation with these men of God. **Truth #196: Without a lifestyle of repentance, a man demonstrates his divorce and estrangement from God, because his decree of unfaithfulness to his moral obligation to be righteous, has been predetermined through the choice of the individual!**

▶ 3. *separation.* **Truth #197: What sanctification is to the saint's separation from the things of this world, carnality is to the self righteous, as a separation from the things of God!** These carnal dogs wanted to separate [to divide and conquer] the move of God among the people. They figured that if they could succeed in sifting Paul and Barnabas from the multitudes, they could retard the work of God.

▶ 4. *to refuse to have anything to do with.* This would also include the refusal to acknowledge, to accept, to support or to fulfill an obligation or pay a debt. Again, as long as a person voluntarily refuses to acknowledge the scriptural truth of his carnality, he won't understand God's righteousness. These Pharisaic Jews obviously possessed no idea of their self righteousness. What was evident to others, was closed to them! Where these Jews were blind and willingly ignorant to the darkness of their own carnality, Paul and Barnabas were enlightened to the knowledge of carnality. **Truth #198: An obvious character trait of the impenitent and the carnally minded, is their refusal to have anything to do with that which contradicts their traditions and/or challenges their carnality!**

▶ 5. *to deny.* When someone is in denial, he or she may exhibit certain behaviourial tendencies that coincide with their denial. An example would be a drunk driver who obviously would be in violation of the law, but as far as he is concerned, he denies his intoxication. How about the person who is told the truth of a matter pertinent to him and because it cuts deep, he baulks at it resorting to emotional outbursts or perhaps violence. These coercive Jews, by their actions and their words, demonstrated their denial of the truth of Scripture; which states that there is no other name under heaven by which men may be saved, for there is salvation in none other! These aversive Jews denied the path of life that leads to salvation from their carnality; (Lie Based Thinking). Sad isn't it, there are those who choose to live like this? Why is that? Because they are addicted to their ignorance. **Truth #199: Without a lifestyle of repentance, denial is to be expected by those who resist the truth of the gospel. Their denial intimates an alternative mind set, that negates reality whether spiritual or physical, for they possess ulterior motives!**

- 6. *an obligation.* The idea of obligation implies *oughtness*. By this I mean that moral obligation is something that we ought to do for the highest good. Nowadays, the societal mind set is the preoccupation of individual rights. For example, the misinterpretation of the right to free speech, intimates that any person may say anything he wants without the threat of incarceration. However, what this person fails to realize is that the freedom of speech applies to that which *ought* to be said, and not to that which should not be said. In other words, profane and vulgar speech is not conducive to a healthy self image or reputation. Neither does it accomplish righteousness. Conversely, that which *ought* to be spoken is first proper and conducive to a positive end.

The fact that societal influence misrepresents freedom and misunderstands the intent and scope of our freedoms [inalienable rights] shows just how far America has regressed from that righteous standard as set forth in the Constitution of the United States! Here then is the irony, *right* is the root word for righteous (ness). When people insist on having their rights, the fact they persist in this only evinces their unrighteousness, thereby validating the truth that people really don't understand righteousness as the Apostle Paul wrote in *Romans 3:10-11*! But this is to be expected since carnality is denied. **Truth #200: The saint seeks after righteousness through a lifestyle of repentance, because repentance is a moral obligation to God, to himself and others as a spiritual discipline of that which ought to be done!**

The Golden Rule of Obligation
Matthew 7:12
"Therefore, all things whatsoever ye would that men should do to you, do ye even so to them: for this is the law and the prophets."

Luke 6:31
"And as ye would that men should do to you, do ye also to them likewise."

There is *a condition of obligation,* which appertains to the existence of humanity. The fact that humanity exists, presupposes the a ground of obligation must also exist, which also presupposes the "golden rule" of obligation. Both justify the highest good as an ultimate end. For example, Scripture teaches that we are our brother's keeper, which denotes that one man ought to esteem another ahead of himself. Since mankind was initially created by Almighty God to glorify Him in their living, due to the fall of Adam and Eve, Almighty God obligated Himself as something He should (ought) to do to reconcile lost humanity back to Himself. He did so through Jesus Christ His Son. *(cf. 2 Cor. 5:19)*

There is *a ground for obligation* also. The difference between the ground *for* obligation and *a condition of obligation* is this: A ground for obligation pertains to a mindful consideration of *oughtness*, which relates to a self awareness that something should or ought to be done. Whereas, a condition of obligation pertains to that which proceeds from this thoughtful consideration, and is made evident by the activity performed or demonstrated as the thing that ought to be done. For example, should a passerby witness an assault, the passerby inherently should have a sense of obligation to do something. So acting on his better judgment of conscience, that sense for the higher good, he acts upon his intuition thereby obligating himself to do something to obtain a desired outcome for the highest good. But it must be said that depending upon the action taken, will determine the outcome of the condition of obligation. For instance, if I happened upon rape attempt, I could run to the aid of the woman or I could shout from a safe distance. If I shout from a safe distance, chances are that my shouting would not rescue the woman. But if I allow myself to become personally involved by physically saving the woman from her intended thugs, I could effectively rescue her from certain harm right then and there. My actions therefore would define the condition of obligation, as being either direct and active or indirect and passive. **Truth #201: A lifestyle of repentance then, is the ground for the obligation as a consideration for salvation which ought to be inherently desired, for God has placed that longing in the heart of every man. Therefore, a lifestyle of repentance is that duty of oughtness, which is that which should be done, to achieve the highest good, namely FREEDOM; salvation from carnal propencities/indulgences.**

7. *to disown.* Before you can disown something, you first

must own it, right? It's the same thing with revival. Before anything may be revived, it first had to vive [live]! These dispossessing Jews, through their actions, basically broadcasted that they had already chosen to disown God and the things of God. This included salvation! You see, Almighty God provided salvation to humanity 2000 years ago on the cross, when He sent His only Begotten Son, Jesus Christ to die on our behalf. Jesus purchased our salvation through His atoning blood, for the remission of our sins. But this is common knowledge. However, what I believe is not commonly known is that the provisions of salvation now belongs to everybody and that this gift of eternal life is ours, just for the asking, for as Jesus Christ, Himself has said, *"Whosoever shall believe on Him, shall not perish but have eternal life." (cf. John 3:15-18)* That is too say we own it! Be that as it may, and as it was then, so it still remains today that whenever a man repudiates God and the things of God, he in effect is disowning [dispossessing] the provisions of salvation, which are already his! Although I have written this work, it still is beyond me as to the grave effects of man's denial of his carnality! For the life of me, I cannot understand why people choose to continue in their repudiations and live out their life in their squalid carnality. **Truth # 202: Without a lifestyle of repentance, a person dispossesses himself of the provisions of his salvation which was given him on the cross of Calvary. With repentance however, the saint retains his salvation and his resurrection shall be the evidence of his reward!**

Hosea 14:1 AMP
"O Israel, return to the Lord your God, for you have stumbled and fallen, [visited by calamity] due to your iniquity [carnality]."

The text verse speaks of a return to the Lord your God. Should you ask anyone within the theater of Christianity, to define repentance to you, the most probable reply would be, *to turn from sin*. That's it! As you the reader have learned thus far, repentance is so much more than that. It's the same ignorance pertaining to God's grace, which most people define as merely *unmerited favor*. The holy angels of God, who encircled His throne, cried out "Holy, Holy, Holy! "*(cf. Is. 6:1-8)* I believe that every time they came full circle, Almighty God revealed to them more of His vastness and majesty. Therefore, since God has no beginning nor end, in that He is the End from the Beginning and the Alpha and the Omega, *(aleph-tav)* it is reasonable to say that all things of God, which have their origin in Him, are also eternal and therefore are so much more than finite man can fathom. So in conclusion, I would like to encourage you to come and allow yourself to return to the Lord your God, for He has torn that He may heal, He has stricken that He may bind. He has provided salvation to one and all. It belongs to you and me as an obligation of God's grace to all of mankind. Don't disown your salvation. Turn from your repudiations and decide for yourself that you will no longer frustrate the grace of God!

Notes:

Chapter 29
Repentance in the Book of Joel

The Rules of Engagement Have Changed

During the 1980s, I was a self defense safety instructor with the California Highway Patrol, while stationed in San Diego, Ca. As a requirement for this position, I had to attend extensive hours of training to acquaint myself with all the physical methods of arrest. This also included a working knowledge of arrest techniques and a level of proficiency with the use of the latest innovation of the standard police baton, the "PR-24." This PR-24 resembled a martial arts weapon, which originated out of Okinawa. Basically, it was a farming instrument used to thrash wheat or barley. Obviously then, this new baton would prove itself a definite improvement over the standard stick baton, used by law enforcement agencies for decades. Now imagine, you and I are farmers and we are thrashing our crops in the heat of the day, when there appears off in the distance, several men on horses approaching at a full gallop. They approach us trampling our fields in total disregard for civility. All you and I have for our defense is our little farming implement (PR-24), which is made of a shorter "yawarwa" handle perpendicularly attached approximately 6 inches from one end of a longer 24 inch thrashing stick. Because the rules of engagement have suddenly changed, that which was an implement of husbandry would now become a weapon to devastate and destroy! The techniques you and I applied to our chores of thrashing has suddenly become the combative tactics of war! **Truth #203: The**

battlefield is our soul. The objective then, is to suppress carnality and the tour of duty is our entire life! Through a lifestyle of repentance, the saint engages in spiritual warfare employing spiritual weaponry and battle tactics to lacerate, shatter, rend and tear his carnality and his entrenched strongholds! As saints of the Most High God, we are that weapon to devastate and to destroy! Our skill and the level of proficiency in the use of the sword of the Spirit (the Word of God) against carnality shall determine our victory or our defeat!

Isaiah 41:15-16
"Behold, I will make you a new sharp threshing instrument which has teeth; you shall thresh the mountains and beat them small, and shall make the hills like chaff. You shall winnow them, and the wind will carry them away, and the tempest and the whirlwind shall scatter them. And you shall rejoice in the Lord, you shall glory in the Holy One of Israel." (cf. Jer. 4:11-13)

Isaiah 54:16-17 AMP
"Behold, I have created the smith who blows on the fire of coals and who produces a weapon for its purpose; and I have created the devastator to destroy. But no weapon that is formed against you shall prosper, and every tongue that shall rise against you in judgment you shall show to be in the wrong. This [peace, righteousness, security, triumph over opposition] is the heritage of the servants of the Lord [those in whom the ideal Servant of the Lord is reproduced]; this is the righteousness or the vindication which they obtain from Me [this is that which I impart to them as their justification], says the Lord."

Consider Adam in the garden of Eden. He knew that there was a snake in the grass, long before Eve encountered it. Adam, it seems, neglected his duty to eliminate the snake, possibly surmising that if the snake wouldn't bother him or Eve, Adam wouldn't bother it. Eventually, the snake did provoke Eve, and Adam found himself in a quagmire. That quagmire being, before he was a gardener, suddenly he became a survivor! And so it continues to be with humanity today. *Every person knows the existence of their own carnality; and yet people choose to either deny it or ignore the cause of it, surmising that they can cope with their selfishness and keep it at bay, only to be betrayed by this covert entity within their soul.* But Almighty God wants His people to grow in knowledge and be established in truth. Where once we lived as children of the devil, now we are to live as a sons and soldiers of God who have been transformed into weapons, to devastate and to destroy the adversaries against our soul!

Awake to Repentance

Joel 1:5-6
"Awake, ye drunkards, and weep; and howl, all ye drinkers of wine, because of the new wine; for it is cut off from your mouth. For a nation has come up upon my land strong, and without number, whose teeth are as the teeth of a lion, and he hath the cheek teeth of a great lion."

Can't you just see it? The shepherd boy David once rebuked the Israeli army for their loitering about, while Goliath taunted them and blasphemed the Lord their God. David charged them, by reminding them of their military obligation and said, "Is there not a cause?" *(cf. 1 Sam. 17:29)* Here, Joel is exhorting the people who have become complacent in their devotion to God to awake to righteousness! Joel preached repentance to an impenitent people. Like the other prophets before him, he too used an actual event to parallel a spiritual truth of judgment. In this, there would be no doubt or misinterpretation as to exactly what his meaning and intent was. It appears that there just ain't no getting around the wickedness of men. I mean, just how many times does humanity have to go around this same mountain? As the text verses indicate, there was a nation which invaded the land.

This invading nation, which came up against the promised land, had the teeth of a lion. This indicates that Almighty God vindicated Himself through the righteous judgment of His chosen people, who were altogether impenitent! Since the land belonged to God, He alone held the title deed. His chosen people were tenants, not squatters, and therefore were to be stewards of God's property. You see, through repentance, the saint has a proper perspective of his own self worth. **Truth #204: Through a lifestyle of repentance, the saint remembers that he is not his own and that Almighty God holds the title deed on his life and all of his material possessions!**

Rend Your Hearts and not Your "holy" Garments
Joel 2:12-13 AMP

*"Therefore also now, says the Lord, turn and **keep on coming to Me** with all your heart, with fasting, with weeping, and with mourning [**until every hindrance is removed** and the broken fellowship is restored]. Rend your hearts and not your garments and return to the Lord, your God, for He is gracious and merciful, slow to anger, and abounding in loving kindness; and He revokes His sentence of evil [when His conditions are met]."* (emphasis mine)

Joel enjoined the people to repent and turn to the Lord their God once again. They were to demonstrate their perpetual penitence through fasting, weeping, and mourning. He told them to rend [tear violently, tear out with violence] their heart [character, conduct and behavior] and not just their garments. **Truth #205: A lifestyle of repentance is a spiritual discipline undertaken by those saints of God, who are of a violent disposition and possess a righteous indignation against their own carnal-**

ity! A passive, cursive and effortless pretense of repentance will be of no benefit, because repentance is a duty and this makes it an obligation for the highest good or end, namely the salvation of the soul!

Matthew 11:12 AMP
"And from the days of John the Baptist until the present time, the kingdom of heaven has endured violent assault, and violent men seize it by force [as a precious prize - a share in the heavenly kingdom is sought with most ardent zeal and intense exertion]."

Torn "holy" Garments

Through the centuries, well meaning church folk have adopted strict codes of dress in an attempt to deter provocative attire among and between the sexes of their congregations. These attempts were and are meant to counteract the influence of carnal tendencies within society which had/has infiltrated the church. Although a code of dress is noble and therefore admirable, it is however, carnal. I say this, because of the extreme measures taken towards unisexism. The result is always a legalistic view of morality and propriety, because a uniform dress code, (holiness clothing) has been reduced to a religious dogma, that intimates a form of *will worship,* which is not scriptural, but could seemingly be based upon some fetish that a particular leader may secretly have regarding an extreme sexual dysfunction. And when one thinks of the several ministers who have fallen off their sanctimonious pedestal, in the past decade of two, due to a sexual penchant, this observation of leadership within a carnal church could reasonably be made.

Through the years, I've engaged in conversation with those who hold to a strict dress code. It seems that the reasons or explanations which they give are predominantly based upon a distorted view point, emphasizing the power of the impropriety rather than accentuating the power of God. Each time, the dialogue was tainted with two little words, "Yea, but..." followed by a nonsensical, emotional postulation spoken by the adherent, which effectively annuls any scriptural truth that I have presented, previously to the "Yea, but." It seems then, that there is a desire to please man and to coddle his carnality rather than God. The end result is always a blanket policy stressed by spiritual leadership, so as to avoid the judgment dilemma. Rather than address the dysfunction within the soul of a leader or to correct those few who are flamboyantly dressed, the majority suffer for the in digressions of a few, all because the leader chooses to avoid the confrontation of judgment!

This method of control could be called a *kangaroo court*, which basically is the disciplinary technique employed to engender control, mastery or unison of a body of people. This applied form of justice unfolds by leaps and bounds, often at the expense of the majority, for the error of just a few. Hence, it is known as a kangaroo court.

(Webster's) Although the leader may not be a tyrant, he is still a dictator! This technique disregards the "due process" of scriptural law and is often found in the ranks of frontier groups or by prison inmates. And this is very fitting since such dogmas incarcerate people into religious observances or worldly compliance, without the benefit of propriety and scriptural understanding.

So often, what is considered appropriate dress for either gender has been determined through the cultural influence of any civilization. For instance, there are folks in the jungles of South America who live their entire lives without a stitch of clothing! Other regions of the globe where people, indigenous to their particular climate, have adopted a code of dress most suitable and appropriate for that climatic condition. Here in western civilization, it is appropriate to wear clothing and depending on the region or work ethic of this northern hemisphere, the articles of clothing may fluctuate from one nation to another. But this is commonly known and history reveals this in civilizations of antiquity.

So why is there such a big stink about a manner of dress among the churches, specifically? Oftentimes, the predetermined dress code of churches is based solely on a self deprecating disposition of the distinctive qualities that naturally exist between a man and a woman, boy or girl. In other words, a unisex appearance is approved of or preferred. Those who practice this, suffer unnecessarily and especially in hot climatic conditions that would warrant a more sensible dress; and to outsiders, the sacrifice caused by compliance to such a dress code, would be considered as being rather odd.

There are some churches which believe in faith alone to heal or cure a physical affliction. However, should the afflicted die, then the leader of this group of people would be run up on charges for negligent homicide, and this unfortunate scenario is not uncommon. Extreme measures are taken by the proponents of this dogma, who generally consider the medical profession unnecessary. Similarly, there are some who might sew long sleeves onto the manufactured short sleeve shirts or sew leggings to manufactured shorts, just to conform to the idle fancies and the nonsensical dictates of carnal men!

I am in full agreement that no one should dress in such a way that is either provocative, erotic, seductive, alluring or suggestive especially in a church assembly. In fact, to be an exhibitionist anywhere is down right improper and immoral! There are elementary schools here in America and in other nations which do have a dress code for their students. Specifically, the Roman Catholic Schools have had such a code for decades. I know! I was raised as a Catholic and had to wear their prescribed clothing. But if clothing alone was the panacea against lustful sins or improprieties and indecency, why then does the Roman Catholic Church have such a problem with the molestation of school age boys who are required to dress as boys? Lately, due to the excessive violence with school gangs and the such, some public schools have also adopted a uniformed dress code for their students in an attempt to deter such violence against other students and teachers. But without the Spirit of God, their carnal attempts shall fail them, because God has long since been expelled from school!

Oftentimes, a manner of dress which a particular church may prefer, is based upon decent apparel which is first modest and then appropriate in an attempt to neutralize the opportunity for temptation and possible adultery or molestation. Come to think of it, with all the recent problems the Roman Catholic Church has had with their homosexual and pedophile priests, validates that even a uniformed dress code is no deterrent against sexual vice!

A compromise should exist in the form of tolerances. Even the military, with its strict uniform regulations have very limited tolerances for the wearing of hair, and the uniform, itself. Apply this to *holiness clothing* and a compromise can be reached, if the leadership will only allow themselves to remit the extremities of zero tolerance, which imprisons the members of their respective congregations.

So having established a general opening argument for holiness clothing, I wish now to investigate the scriptural support and basis for some misinterpretations concerning clothing and misinformed mythologies of carnal men. I'll begin with this statement. Based upon my cursive research, the Bible does not say anything regarding *holiness clothing* outside of the required garments pertaining to the high priest!

Cross Dressers and Switch Hitters Are an Abomination
Genesis 1:27
"So God created man in His own image, in the image and likeness of God He created him; male and female He created them." (cf. Gen. 2:21-25)

Deuteronomy 22:5 AMP
"The women shall not wear that which pertains to a man, neither shall the man put on a woman's garment, for all that do so are an abomination to the Lord your God."

Deuteronomy 23:1 AMP
"He who is wounded in the testicles, or has been made a eunuch, shall not enter into the congregation of the Lord." (cf. Mat. 19:11-12)

In these three verses, Almighty God has established a distinction between the sexes. He does not hide or attempt to conceal any natural quality of either gender. Excluding *Genesis 1:27*, Creator God only commands that men must wear men's clothing and that women are to wear women's clothing.(This would include cosmetics and jewelry.) That's it! But what or who determines clothing for either gender? I don't see any definitive declaration whatsoever. What I do see, is that men are to wear clothing so designated as men's garments (by society) and the same is true of the women.

Cross dressers, switch hitters and certain risque' establishments, radio personalities and sports figures who are renown for their deviate patronage, manner of dress and accompanying lifestyle would be of this abominable category, even to the point of taking hormonal injections or surgically removing their genitalia to alter their physical appearance! When I was an active law enforcement officer, I had numerous occasions to arrest "switch hitters" and "cross dressers" from the streets of San Diego. Although these men were male physically, their effeminate character traits and their altered appearance portrayed that of a whore.

Shearing Stress of Carnality

1 Corinthians 11:5-6 AMP
"And any woman who [publicly] prays or prophecies (teaches,

refutes, reproves, admonishes, or comforts) when she is bareheaded dishonors her head (her husband): it is the same as [if her head were] **shaved**. For if a woman will not wear [a head] covering, then she should cut off her hair too; but if it is disgraceful for a woman to have her head **shorn (to shear by cutting short) or shaven,** let her cover [her head]." (emphasis mine)

1 Corinthians 11:13-16 AMP
"Consider for yourselves; is it proper and decent [according to your customs] for a woman to offer up prayer to God [publicly] with her head uncovered? **Does not the native sense of propriety (experience, common sense, reason) itself** teach that for a man to wear long hair is a dishonor [humiliating and degrading] to Him, But if a woman has long hair, it is her ornament and glory? For her hair is given to her for a covering. **Now if anyone is disposed to be argumentative and contentious about this,** we hold to and recognize no other custom [in worship] than this, nor do the churches of God, generally." (emphasis mine)

Paul compared a woman's short hair to a shorn or shaved head! The word *shorn* means, "to shear." *Shear* means, "to cut close, trim" among other things. With regards to the Pentecostal bun, Scripture states that women are to *customarily* wear their hair long as a covering, which denotes a veil of submission to her husband. Research has shown that it was *customary* for the men to wear their hair cut close and short throughout history, and that the women wore their hair long. Therefore, customarily, for a woman to wear her hair up *high* and *tight* as in a bun, could denote a desire for a change of venue with regards to God's established order of things. The result of which is the occurrence of a *shearing stress* that could insinuate a usurpation of authority or superiority, as well as a shaved head! According to Webster's, *Shearing Stress* means, "A force causing two contacting parts or layers to slide upon each other, in opposite directions parallel to the plane of their contact." This also implies that friction would exist between any two objects as a result of such action. **Truth #206: The friction caused by the shearing stress of carnality against the intended order of righteousness, is eliminated through a lifestyle of repentance!**

To understand shearing stress, consider the cumulus cloud tops of approaching thunderstorms. When these cloud tops are seen as extended vapor trails behind the cloud base, that trailing edge shows that a high velocity, opposing cross wind, at that altitude, has sheared the storm front and its cloud tops with *wind shear*. This wind shear prevents the cyclonic cloud formations necessary for the organization of hurricanes and tornados, and that is why Meteorologists call it, "Wind Shear." *So when women choose to wear her hair short, or when men choose to wear women's garments, then they in effect are creating a shearing stress against the prevailing order of masculinity and femininity, because the velocity of their carnal, wind shear is in direct opposition to established order!*

The reason that the Apostle Paul addressed this was due to the fact that in the city of Corinth, the high priestess and all her female priestesses portrayed themselves as men in their idol worship of Aphrodite, their goddess of love. Research has also shown that these women wore their hair in a "butch" fashion thereby representing men, who wore their hair short. Additionally, the high priestess would also wear military armament, which further portrayed her as a man and that she would engage in rehearsed sexual dances with the subservient priestesses. Consequently, while on his second missionary journey, Paul observed these pagan customs which were culturally accepted by the citizens of this Grecian city. Paul, who was always observant of others, recognized that these pagan practices were common place, and that everyone citizen had a common knowledge about these temple deviations and sexual tangents. I wouldn't be surprised, if the Christians then dressed in a manner which resembled their pagan culture. So when he addressed the Corinthian Christians, he spoke of that of which they were already familiar with, to that which they were unfamiliar too. So contextually speaking, since their culture was pagan and immoral, Paul stressed to them that which is first decent, proper and reasonable as a righteous alternative to that which was pagan and immoral. And the spiritual application may be extended to our society today. Paul said in *1 Corinthians 11:1, "Pattern yourselves after me as I imitate and follow Christ."* Why would Paul open with this statement? The reason he did was that for centuries, the Grecian culture of pagan worship was that example of life, and the people had long since patterned their living according to this customary immorality. So Paul said, "Pattern yourselves after me, as I follow after Christ" thereby teaching a righteous alternative lifestyle to live. In effect, Paul gave them another option or choice upon which to follow after, for he knew that one choice was no choice. The fact that he taught the citizens of Corinth righteousness, further substantiates that righteousness must be taught, for how else shall anyone understand righteousness?

As a final comment about the deviate manner of dress and appearance, based upon the historical pagan facts just mentioned, it seems then that when a woman wears her "bun" with her hair high and tight, the appearance of her head looks as if her hair had been sheared or shaved, just as the high priestess wore hers! But I say this as a man. **Truth #207: Holiness clothing is an external deviate dress code, to that which is flesh and temporal. Since no man is to know another according to the flesh, it is reasonable to reject such nonsensical postulations of disturbed men!** *(cf. 2 Cor. 5:16)*

Another Man's Scruples

1 Corinthians 10:27-29 AMP
"In case one of the unbelievers invites you to a meal and you

want to go, eat whatever is served you without examining into its source because of conscientious scruples. But if someone tells you, This has been offered in sacrifice to an idol, do not eat it, out of consideration for the person who informed you, and for conscience's sake, I mean for the sake of his conscience, not yours, [do not eat it]. For why should **another man's scruples** apply to me and my liberty of action be determined by his conscience?" (emphasis mine)

> Romans 14:22-23 AMP
> "Your personal convictions [on such matters] exercise [them] as in God's presence, keeping them to yourself [striving only to know the truth and obey His will]. Blessed (happy, to be envied) is he who has no reason to judge himself for what he approves [who does not convict himself by what he chooses to do. But the man who has doubts (misgivings, an uneasy conscience) about eating, and then eats [perhaps because of you], stands condemned [before God], because he is not true to his convictions and he does not act from faith."

Humanity stands naked and exposed to Almighty God! (*cf.* Heb. 4:13) Therefore, man's culture must determine for his society the appropriate manner of dress for its citizens. To allow another to influence or otherwise impose his convictions upon you is flat out wrong, scripturally speaking. Having said this, it would not be a violation of Scripture to broaden the spiritual significance of food and drink as these two passages refer, and apply them to a specified dress code, or to wear such articles in a seductive manner, as is the case today.

The idea that holiness clothing is a religious mandate is utter nonsense, out side of that attire which is altogether decent and proper. Specifically, this dogmatic influence has been that women should wear their hair in a bun, and that women where not to wear shorts, skirts or pants, or the men were not to wear shorts either; but were to wear at all times and in all activities trousers regardless of heat, chores or sport activity. The Bible does not address this whatsoever! Neither does it say that cosmetics are not to be worn or applied. It does however say, that it is an abomination to God for men to wear that which pertains to women and for a women to wear that which pertains to men!

Colossians 2:8 AMP
"See to it that no one carries you off as spoil or makes you yourselves captive by his so called philosophy and intellectualism and vain deceit (idle fancies and plain nonsense), following human tradition (men's ideas of the material rather the spiritual world), just crude notions following the rudimentary and elementary teachings of the universe and disregarding [the teachings of] Christ (the Messiah)."

Binding and Loosing

Matthew 16:19 AMP
"I will give you the keys of the kingdom of heaven; and whatever you bind (declare to be improper and unlawful) on earth must be whatever is bound in heaven; and whatever you loose (declare lawful) on earth must be what is already loosed in heaven." (cf. Is. 22:22)

With regards to rending one's heart, what comes to mind is the spiritual weaponry of binding and loosing. Specifically, the Greek word *deo* comes from the root word, *deomani* which means, "to beg as in binding oneself to a petition, beseech, make a request, and pray." This research reveals that the word, *bind* has more applications to it than just binding some iniquitous thought, (Lie Based Thinking). Furthermore, the word *loose* comes from the Greek word *luo*. It means, "to loosen, break up, destroy, dissolve, unloose, melt and put off." *Luo* is related to the Greek words *rhegnumi* and *agnumi* which means, "to break, wreck, crack to sunder by separation of its parts, shatter to minute fragments, disrupt, lacerate, convulse, burst, rend and tear."

Joel conveyed God's explicit will to see His people engage in spiritual warfare as in a military campaign, because the rules of engagement have changed! They were to do this, by binding the iniquitous thoughts of their carnal mind to the Mind of the Spirit of God, and to loosen the blinding veils caused by their Lie Based Thinking, that they would behold the light and the image of the glorious gospel, *(cf. Heb. 1:1, 2:1-4)* which is the image of Jesus Christ. *(cf. 2 Cor. 4:4)* **Truth #208: Through a lifestyle of repentance, the methods applied to binding and loosing may be summed up in just one simple technique. Simply put, the saint binds the spirit of his mind to the Spirit of the Mind of Christ. And he loosens the Lie Based Thinking of the spirit of his carnal mind, as he loosens the charges that are his in and through the Mind of Christ!**

Create a Faith Environment for God to Move

Repentance teaches the saint to create for himself a faith environment in which Almighty God can move, because repentance is based upon faith in Christ, for without faith, why should anyone repent? In these closing days of the last days before the day of God's wrath, which He is about to pour out as His righteous judgment upon this unrighteous world, there must be a sense of urgency and a desperation that only comes through a lifestyle of repentance! This degree of repentance, denotes a level of travail that is first aggressive and down right hostile against the ravages of carnality within one's soul. Mind you, you will get bloody in the spirit! It is for this reason that the prophets of old hammered home the preaching of righteousness. As it was then, so it still remains today that although times may change, people really don't. Therefore, repentance must be preached today to an unrighteous world and a carnal church!

A saint's triumphant life in God is his reward, due to his overcoming in and throughout his life. The victory that overcomes is obtained in, by and through *faith and repentance, for they are the cohesive partners in one's salvation,* and as in any warfare, the saint will get bloody in the spirit! The faith environment he creates for himself, will transform the battlefield before him. Therefore the saint, as a good soldier who has endured hardships and as a man of faith, is also a man of mettle. That is, he has within him, as an ingredient of God, faith, which is that ingrained capacity for meeting stress or strain with fortitude and resilience! Just as, the ambient conditions and temperatures of a sun filled day are warmth, brightness, energy and power, likewise, this environment of faith created, produces the very same climatic conditions in which Almighty God is allowed to move and the saint experiences. **Truth #209: Just as a movie director creates an environment that liberates the actor to express himself freely, likewise, the environment created through faith and repentance which the saint creates for himself, liberates the Holy Ghost within him to express Himself through the saint, as he is God's mouthpiece!**

Chapter 30
Repentance in the Book of Amos

Establish Judgment at the Gates
Amos 5:15 AMP
"Hate the evil and love the good and establish judgment in the [court of the city's] gate. It may be that the Lord, the God of hosts, will be gracious to the remnant of Joseph [the northern kingdom]." (brackets mine)

The Prophet Amos exhorted the prosperous people of his day to repent. He said, "Hate the evil and love the good and establish judgment in the gate..." Herein was the problem; there was no righteous judgment against the prosperity of wickedness within a flourishing nation! Judgment, as a fortress, must be established in the gates of the carnal mind otherwise, moral depravity thrives within society as a whole. The county seats, the chamber of commerce, city councils, state capitals, a nation's capital, even the heads of households exist to establish judgment in the gates of society. So the question is what sort of gate are you; or are you a hinge plate bolted to the framework of your carnality? Any gate is a barricade and any hinge plate is not. Through righteous judgment, defenses are established as safe guards against carnality. The gate restricts the encroachment of vermin from without, and at the same time, protects those within from infiltration of external influences. A hinge plate serves the gate in that the gate is fastened to the hinge plate, which enables the gate/door to swing open or closed. **Truth #210: A man lacking godliness, sits back bolted to the framework of his carnality and intentionally watches and purposely allows all manner of influences free passage into his heart, his home and his society! When this occurs, then the gate is in need of repair.**

The gate spoken of in Amos, was the actual location from which major decisions were made for the best interests of the populace and the land. It also represented the resolutions that pertained to specified branches of government, such as the legislative and the judicial. It was also from this gate that the city fathers established a defense, as constructed fortification for the city, against intruders as well as to enact laws for the good of society. **Truth #211: A lifestyle of repentance establishes righteous judgment against carnality within the gates of the mind, thereby undergirding the branches of the heart and soul with faith quality decisions. Therefore, repentance possesses a lawfulness as a decision, from the executive faculty of the will, as a resolute judgment made for the soul and against carnality!** Consequently, the saint becomes a shield as that gate or door, when he executes God's Word! Since any door is generally larger than a man to allow easy and safe passage, likewise the enlarged heart of a saint is also greater than he, for greater is He that is in you, than he that is in the world.

From the standpoint of a shield as any gate is, the Roman shield was as large as the man carrying it. This shield was a very versatile piece of armament, because it was so designed to interlock with other shields and together these shields protected the Roman soldiers from injury as they advanced their position across the battlefield toward their enemy. In fact, these soldiers often engraved the names and dates of their previous military campaigns which they survived, on the back side of their shield. These engravings were a constant reminder to them of their valor and might in victories past.

The point being that those who know the Lord their God, shall be strong and do exploits for God. Almighty God would have His saints to remind themselves of their past accomplishments with Him.

Repentance Postpones God's Judgment

Truth #212: A lifestyle of repentance postpones God's judgment! It was for this reason that Amos preached repentance to his fellow citizens. Yet, they would not listen! God has always warned the world of coming judgments. However, history has shown that His judgments did fall, because impenitence ushered it in on the coattails of man's carnality. He warned Noah of the coming flood *(Gen. 6:13)*; Abraham and Lot of the destruction of Sodom *(Gen. 18:17, 19:14)*; Joseph of the seven-year famine *(Gen. 41:30)*; Moses of the ten plagues on Egypt *(Ex. 7:1)*; Jonah of the destruction of Nineveh *(Jon. 1:2, 3:4)*; Amos of the downfall of Syria, Philistia, Tyre, Edom, Ammon, Moab, Judah, and Israel *(Amos 1 and 2)*.

Many other prophets received detail revelations about the final events in connection with *our carnality* or the *sin element* (iniquitous thoughts preceding Lie Based Thinking) of the chosen people, and in every case the warnings went unheeded! Consequently, righteous judgment was suddenly and abruptly executed. Jonah announced the destruction of Nineveh, but judgment was postponed following a city wide repentance. However, when later generations of Ninevites eventually backslided and returned to extreme wickedness, the warnings of Nahum, the Prophet, were carried out completely against them.

Christ's coming was also foretold throughout the Old Testament, from Genesis to Malachi. These Messianic Prophecies, as well as the judgments to come, are the substance of the prophetic word spoken. As they come to pass, as some have already, then the fulfillment of the prophetic word articulated, shall be the evidence of the word of faith spoken! *(cf. Heb. 11:1)* These fulfilled judgments and of those to come, are the warnings of Jesus and of the prophets concerning the future, that as each day comes and goes, God's judgments wax closer to every inhabitant and nation on earth. *(cf. Is. 26:9, 30:8)*

Of interest are the judgments, which God levied against the surrounding nations of Israel for their wickedness. Since Almighty God did judge these neighboring nations to Israel, it stands to reason then that Almighty God would have to eventually judge Israel! *(cf. Amos 1 and 2)* In other words, the traditional church today must realize that it is inevitable that Almighty God must judge an unrighteous world and a defiled church. Therefore, He must judge His own house! Just because prosperity and religion exist within the worldly church is no deterrent against God's judgment! If anything, such worldliness will attract God's judgment, like an insect that is drawn to a bug light!

Ezekiel 18:30 AMP
"Therefore, I will judge you, O house of Israel, everyone according to his ways, says the Lord God. Repent and turn from all your transgressions, **lest iniquity be your ruin** *and so shall they not be a stumbling block to you."* (emphasis mine)

Revelation 3:5 AMP
"Remember then from what heights you have fallen. Repent (change the inner man to meet God's will) and do the works you did previously [when first you knew the Lord], or else I will visit you and remove your lamp stand from its place, unless you change your mind and repent."

To Seek Means to Activate Litigation

Amos exhorts the people towards repentance in chapter five. There are several verses which exhort the people to seek the

Lord their God and righteousness. Specifically, verses 4, 6, 8, 14. Here, the word *seek* means, "to search out, to frequent, to ask or inquire." As applied to law seek means,"*to activate litigation, of all sorts. Be it a lawsuit, prosecution, pleadings, summons, arraignments, depositions, etc.*"(Strong's Concordance Hebrew ref. #1875, page 31)

The Apostle Paul said, "that there is none righteous, no not one; there is none that understands [righteousness as a means to litigate] there is none that seek after God." *(cf. Rom. 3:10-11)* Paul, like Amos exhorted the people of his day to acknowledge their carnality and to seek after righteousness. Obviously then, although times will change, carnally minded people really don't. *It is therefore imperative that humanity must learn righteousness, as a means of litigation.* Amos chapter 3, speaks of the necessity of God's judgment upon impenitent humanity, and in chapter 3 of Romans, Paul speaks of a righteous deficit among the people of his day and within the church! By necessity, judgment is consequently inevitable. And since God's judgments are unavoidable, then it is apparent, that impenitent humanity has been the impetus of this divine edict, all because people refuse to learn the value of righteousness, judicially! **Truth #213: A lifestyle of repentance then, is to seek divine litigation as prosecution to mitigate [suppress] carnality that we might live uprightly!**

Navy S.E.A.L. (Sea, Air and Land)

Amos 9:13

"Behold, the days come, saith the Lord, that the plowman shall overtake the reaper, and the treader of grapes him that soweth seed; and the mountains shall drop sweet wine, and all the hills shall melt."

Taking the first half of this verse, I would like to compare the plowman as he who walks northbound behind the southbound end of a slow, but strong northbound ox, which is harnessed to a yoke that is plowing [tilling] the soil; and the treader of grapes as he who is marking time, for he is the one who is marching in place and going nowhere fast. I remember the Navy SEAL teams training on the shores of Coronado Island in San Diego, California. These young men were put through the wringer physically, mentally and emotionally! Specifically, I did often observe their training and would watch them carry their heavy floatation devices [rafts] over their heads or on their shoulders into the churning surf and either swim alongside or paddle their rafts out into the ocean swells to a designated turn around point and back again up onto the sandy beach, in formation of course! As fatigued as they were, the more robust trainees would dare not quit. Often the stragglers would have to take another lap or two, just for good measure. Now imagine if you will, a sudden burst of energy that swells up within these stragglers, so much so that they actually catch up with the main formation and out pace them! Like a second wind, a lifestyle of repentance positions us to run from behind in this race called life and win big! Therefore, the plowman is the penitent saint whose walk of faith enables him to overtake the reaper of the harvest unlike those who are persuaded that faith alone, without repentance, (works of righteousness) is all that is necessary for salvation.

The flash in the pan minister or ministry may appear on public television and be coddled by his host, seemingly to portray that he, as the guest, has arrived to the big league; but the saint who is first righteous and has disciplined his heart through repentance, shall be foremost with the Lord God, because he has harnessed his carnality, and has subsequently learned to walk uprightly before God in his integrity. But, the flash in the pan minister or ministry will peter out.

The Treader of Grapes and the Winepress of God

Marking time is a military term. It is a simple drill movement in which a platoon, company or squad of troops will march in place and in unison. Literally, these troops pound the ground with no forward movement. The treader of grapes is basically doing the same thing. Although he may move about in a vat or a winepress trampling the grape, he too goes nowhere fast. Like Samson who pushed the mill wheel around and around, or the person who seems to be stuck in life and is wearied of the grind of his daily, innocuous lifestyle, he treads on. Burdened with only this single task at hand or should I say underfoot, the treader has nothing more to preoccupy himself with. Unlike the busy body who hurries here or there consumed with the sour grapes of self indulgence, and the temporal things of life, the treader is able to contemplate the good grape of his life. He who treads grapes is not mindful and troubled about with so many things, but he is preoccupied with that which is good. *(cf. Lk. 10:38-42)* **Truth #214: A lifestyle of repentance is like the trampling of good grapes, because the saint marks time in place contemplating his life and scrutinizing the sour grape of his carnality! This then is the good part of godliness, because the blood that flows from the grape (fruit) of a consecrated life, is the goodness of Christlikeness which is the best portrayal of God Himself!**

Scripture also speaks of He who treads out the blood of the grapes in the winepress of the wrath of God, whose blood reaches to the bridles of horses. *(cf. Joel 3:13; Rev. 14:18-20)* These verses teach that unless the individual tread out the grapes in his own life, while he lives, then Almighty God will see to it that the carnal man will be trampled underfoot and subsequently crushed by God in the winepress of His judgment! Once again, Scripture teaches that either way, it's all about righteous judgment! The text verse also implies that the treader of grapes shall overtake the sower who sows the seed.

Of interest, is the word *Gethsemane*. It means, "oil press." (Strong's Exhaustive Concordance, Grk. ref. #1068, page 20) However, it also means, "wine-press, shine, oily, wax fat, grease, richness, anointing, plenteous, fruitful, ointment." (Strong's Exhaustive Concordance Heb. ref. #8080, 8081, page 118) The implication of these definitions portrays Jesus Christ, who often prayed in the garden of Gethsemane, which represents for the church a crushing of her carnality and a yielding to His righteousness. Like the *Ma'lach* [to rub, anointing] and the *Ma' shach* [to rub salt into, anointing], the pressing of grapes is also the application of God's anointing, for the fruit of righteousness begets the fruit of the Spirit!

Again of interest is the word *Gath*, which is an ancient Philistine city. It means, "to tread out the grapes, a vat or a wine press for holding the grapes in pressing them. (Strong's Exhaustive Concordance, Heb. ref. #1661, 1660, page 29) Presently, the Palestinian uprising and their terror tactics against Israeli citizens exist to seemingly press the extermination of Israel. In fact, one Palestinian leader said in essence, that his people would not rest until Israel is pushed into the sea and ceases to exist as a nation. This confirms Scripture, which states that the kingdom of heaven suffers violence and the violent take it by force! *(cf. Mat. 11:12)* Whether the *force* of righteousness or the *oppression* of carnality, force is the predominant motivation, and the sooner the saints of God learn this, the sooner they will enjoy the victory over their carnality. **Truth #215: Therefore, a lifestyle of repentance is the pressing force that crushes the sour grape of one's carnality so that the saint will not be lost in the sea of forgetfulness or perish in the lake of fire!**

In the natural order of things, there is seed, time and harvest. According to the seasons such planting and harvesting occurs. However, through a display of God's grace and mercy, the fruit [those who are righteous] will precede the seed [those who are self righteous], because Almighty God reserves the right to intervene and alter the natural order of things. Why? Because penitent humanity [His remnant] will have finally learned the litigation aspects of righteousness and will have met God's terms and conditions for salvation; whereas, the self righteous will live to suffer the consequences of their sin!

Portraits of Travail

Like the penitent inmate who lives out his sentence behind bars, or the men and women who are employed in emergency services, as well as all the men and women of the U.S. Armed Forces, are what I believe to be portraits to humanity of what God means by the travail of the soul. These personnel are ready, at a moments notice, to go to war anywhere in the earth on behalf of America and are ready, at the drop of a hat, to respond to domestic emergency situations. Even the specially trained K-9, will sniff out the scent of rotting flesh and dig frantically to rescue those who have fallen and are buried by debris. They are sent in our place, fighting on our behalf! Likewise, through a lifestyle of repentance, the saint who laments the condition of his nation's abominations, fights on behalf of others for he or she has purposed in his/her heart to be sent as on a mission. **Truth #216: Through a lifestyle of repentance, the saint grieves not the Holy Ghost, because the saints of God have been sealed unto the day of redemption, since they willingly rend their hearts on behalf of others!** Like the rescuers of those who perished on September 11th, 2001, these heroic people have willingly placed themselves in harm's way on behalf of those fallen and their survivors. **Truth #217: Through a lifestyle of repentance, the saint willingly places himself in harm's way, so that he may deprive his carnality of its self indulgences. In doing so, he recovers that which was once dead within him, because he has a nose for it!**

Luke 9:24 AMP
"For whoever would preserve his life and save it will lose and destroy it, but whoever loses his life for My sake , he will preserve and save it [from the penalty of eternal death]."

John 15:13 AMP
"No one has greater love [no one has shown stronger affection] than to lay down (give up) his own life for his friends."

The Identity of the Seal

Our weapons are of the Spirit. They are not carnal, flesh or physical. Since Jesus Christ shed His blood on Calvary's cross, He became bloody physically, for you and me. *God intends for His saints to get bloody in the spirit also.* Like the rigorous training of the military, these blood baths represent to us spiritual training throughout our lifetime. Should the time ever come for actual bloodshed, then God shall provide His grace, that provision from His throne, to endure hardships, even death, unto the end! *Ephesians 1:13* says in essence that the true saints of God have been sealed with the Holy Spirit of promise, because they have been obedient to God's commands. *Ephesians 4:30* says that the saints of God are not to grieve the Holy Spirit, whereby they are sealed unto the day of redemption. Now look at this!

Ezekiel 9:4-6
"And the Lord said unto him, Go through the midst of the city, through the midst of Jerusalem, and set a mark [seal] upon the foreheads of the men that sigh and that cry for the abominations that be done in the midst thereof. And to the others he said in mine hearing, Go ye after him through out the city, and smite: let not your eye spare, neither have pity: Slay utterly old and young, both maids and little children and women, but come not near any man upon whom is the mark; and begin at my sanctuary..." (brackets mine)

Romans 4:11 AMP
"He received a mark [seal] of circumcision as a token or an evidence [and] **seal of righteousness** *which he had by faith while he was still uncircumcised [faith] so that he was to be made the father of all who truly believe..."* (emphasis mine)

In *Romans 4:11*, God identifies the seal spoken of in *Ezekiel 9:4-6*! It's the seal of righteousness through faith! **Truth #218: Therefore, in faith and through a lifestyle of repentance the saint is sealed, because he obeys God's Word, complies to His will, and conforms his life to God's ways!** He receives God's seal of righteousness, because he lives uprightly with integrity before God. Consequently, he is marked for salvation by God!

Repentance as a "Stay of Execution"

Amos 5:14-15
"Seek the good and hate the evil, that ye may live... Hate the evil, and love the good, and establish judgment in the gate, it may be that the Lord God of hosts will be gracious unto the remnant of Joseph [northern kingdom of Israel]." (brackets mine)

Almighty God would never ask us to do something that He himself has not already done. The closing phrase of *Ezekiel 9:6* tells us this and what a powerful revelation this is about repentance! *We repent for ourselves, because we are the house of God, but we do repentance on behalf of others in demonstration of God's love.* Lamenting for the wicked, travailing for the abominations committed all around, weeping over the sin and fasting and travailing for God's mercy, that He would stay His hand of execution against impenitent humanity are all methods of intercession within a lifestyle of repentance.

It has been said, that the business side of the Gospel is souls. I agree with this, however the souls spoken of also include the unregenerate souls already existing within the church! On the one hand, souls represents a head count; but on the other, souls represent the carnal church! Therefore, these attributes of repentance are most needful within the worldly church, for they are synonymous with righteousness, holiness, godliness and sanctification. **Truth #219: A lifestyle of repentance is the saint's intercession and petition, for it is his litigation as a request for a stay of execution!**

Final Appeals for a "Stay of Execution"
John 16:7-11
"Nevertheless, I tell you the truth; it is expedient for you that I go away: for if I go not away, the Comforter will not come unto you; but if I depart, I will send Him unto you. And when He is come, he will reprove the world of sin, and of righteousness, and of judgment: Of sin, because they believe not on me; of righteousness, because I go to my father; and of judgment, ***because the prince of this world is judged.****"* (emphasis mine)

Jesus Christ spoke to His disciples of the office and person of the Holy Spirit [Comforter] which was to arrive after His departure. Specifically, in verses 8 and 11, we read that the Comforter would come to reprove the world of judgment, because the prince of this world is judged [already]. Folks, the devil is just about out of time! He has but a few more appeals to "Stay his Execution!" The calendar date of his demise is just a calender flip away! You see, as long as abominations and all the rest exist within humanity, the devil continues to present his case before Almighty God. No wonder he is the accuser of the brethren! *(cf. Job 1:6, 2:1)* He says to God, "Lord! Its not fair that You have judged me and sentenced me to the lake of fire and brimstone, when all Your so-called chosen people and saints are just as guilty as I!" I can just hear the response from the Lord God.

"You know Satan, you're absolutely correct; It's not fair! What is fair for them has nothing to do with what is fair for you!" And with the slamming of the gavel, the Lord states, "My fairness has nothing to do with My favor, but it has everything to do with justice! Case closed! Next case!"

Only Those on Death Row Know

Death row convicts, reside in a separate facility from the rest of the prison population. Everyone there knows about death row. Especially, those who have been condemned to die! Eventually, with the flip of the calendar, the specified date arrives. The condemned convict has but just a few short hours remaining, before his time for departure arrives. The convict is fully aware of just how and when his demise will occur. With the flip of an electrical switch or the injection of certain chemicals which induce sleep and then heart failure, the convict departs. Unfortunately, mankind, as a whole, has no idea of the manner and time of his demise. Why? Because man refuses to repent and turn from his wicked ways! Therefore, he remains ignorant of his latter end. *(cf. Deut. 32:29; Lk. 12:15-22)* **Truth #220: Through a lifestyle of repentance, the saint becomes very much aware of his mortality and his vulnerability!** Like the prisoner who occupies his cell of penitence, the saint must also occupy a special place in God's heart, for He has sealed him not unto death and damnation, but unto eternal life!

Prisonization and Institutionalization

Prisonization is a term used within the prison system. Psychologically, it basically speaks of the institutional effects upon an inmate who has been in the correctional facility for an extended period of time. The end result being, the inmate becomes *institutionalized. Institutionalization* is another term used in the correctional industry, which denotes that the institutionalized effects upon an inmate interferes with the societal goals of his rehabilitation. Consequently, as any prison is a microcosm of the underground culture of society, so too then is any church a cross section of an open community. Therefore, just as *institutionalization* interferes with rehabilitation likewise, religion, in all its aspects, encumbers reconciliation! Because the common psychological effects in both appertains towards the spirit of the mind. It is safe to say that when a person's mind is renewed, regardless of his circumstance or condition externally, then his soul's regeneration will provide his restoration!

The Absence of Righteous Judgment
Amos 5:21-24 AMP
"I hate, despise your feasts, and I will not smell a savor or take delight in your solemn assemblies. Though you offer Me your burnt offerings, I will not accept them, neither will I look upon them, neither will I look upon the peace or thank offerings of your fatted beasts. **Take away form Me the noise of your songs, for I will not listen to the melody of your harps. But let justice run down like waters and righteousness as a mighty and ever-flowing stream."* (emphasis mine)

Amos identifies repentance primarily as seeking after God, and specifically, God's utter displeasure with man's carnal tradition of self righteousness and his vain oblations. Particularly, the absence of righteousness and judgment. Without righteousness and judgment applied towards carnality, there remains no remedy for man's carnal tragedy. The current state of the worldly church, chronicles the deplorable condition of wickedness among the chosen people in the days of Amos. Back then, society was thriving, the economy was growing and the people enjoyed the good life, independent of God. Their solemn assemblies were mega-congregations and they all prospered. Why?

Because the spiritual leaders of their day prophesied blessings as a judgment for the flesh, but avoided the preaching of righteousness, as a judgment against their carnality! Sounds like the modern church doesn't it? But what really stands out is the statement that God makes through the prophet, "Take away from Me the noise of your songs and the melody of your harps!" It seems that their music, although most eloquent for praise, was very displeasing to God. Probably, because it hinged on entertainment and its lyrics omitted the weightier matters of atonement. I wonder just how much of our praise and worship is just as displeasing to Him? More and more it seems that songs of and about the blood have been replaced with melodies of blessings and promises, once again omitting the weightier matters of atonement [righteousness, holiness]. You see, entertainment diverts the impenitent soul from his obligation to judge his carnality and repent. Since this is the case, then all the songs ever sung or composed could never avert the judgment of God upon a carnal, worldly church! Moreover, every man has a song to sing! Specifically, the song of his character, whether righteous or not, is heard by others. So whatever a man is internally, that heart condition is the song which God hears and sees, for He knows the hearts of all men. Like the cardiologist, Almighty God is a heart specialist and He wants His saints to become His assistants in the operation of righteousness as well.

Workers of Righteousness

The Apostle Peter, told the early church that if there be anyone who is a worker of righteousness, that one would be accepted of God. *(cf. Acts 10:35)* To be a worker of righteousness then is to live a lifestyle of repentance! In this capacity, the saint shall walk in his uprightness before a just and righteous God. Man's neglect fosters God's intervention to execute judgment and righteousness since humanity won't! **Truth #221: A lifestyle of**

repentance then, is a work of righteousness and therefore is a walk of faith to execute judgment upon our own carnality! *(cf. 1 Cor. 11:29-31; 2 Cor. 5:7)*

There are forty-seven prophets whose names appear in Scripture. Most are not known however. Only seventeen prophets are generally known, since individual books are attributed to them by name. All prophets were however, workers of righteousness. Whether they preached it or urged a nation or a king to it, all prophets demonstrated a lifestyle of repentance. They had to, if they were to be true to their calling and office. In these many examples of Scripture, it is reasonable to presume from this preponderance of evidence that a lifestyle of repentance is a qualification of office and a calling to that office. No matter what their names or the times in which they lived, these prophets were united in their testimony. *(cf. Lk. 1:70; Acts 3:21, 24; 2 Pet. 3:2)* Regarding Daniel, he told King Nebuchadnezzar to break off his sins by doing righteousness and by showing mercy. Likewise Amos told an apostate people to do the same. **Truth #222: A lifestyle of repentance then, is a counter measure against the corruption in this world and within ourselves. Therefore, righteousness, like salt, is the preservative of the saint's virtue of holiness!**

Chapter 31
Repentance in the Book of Obadiah

Whenever carnal man fails to give glory and honor to Almighty God in and through the gifts, talents and abilities given him by God, he becomes accursed! This is due to the fact that these consecrated endowments have been abused and misused to glorify man instead of God. In effect, man has neglected God by not catering to the desires of God's pleasure.

Just Who was Esau, Anyway?
Obediah 1:6-7 AMP
"How are the things of Esau [Edom] searched out! How are his hidden treasures sought out! All the men of your confederacy (your allies) have brought you on your way, even to the border; the men who were at peace with you have deceived you and prevailed against you; they who eat your bread have laid a snare under you. **There is no understanding** *[in Edom, or] of it."* (emphasis mine)

Generally, Esau was the eldest son of Isaac and a twin to his brother Jacob. A hairy man, Esau was also a hunter. He was impulsive and prone to emotional outbursts since his carnal tendencies dominated his life. He married at least two Canaanite women without the blessings of his parents, Isaac and Rebecca. These unapproved marriages resulted in a contractual agreement between two other heathen nations with Israel. Esau's selfish character, eventually led to the event when he forfeited his birthright to Jacob over a plate of porridge. As a result, Esau hated his brother Jacob, even to the point of murder. This threat forced Jacob to flee for his life, who was absent twenty-one years before he returned to his family.

Throughout his life, Esau found no place of repentance, for his heart was filled with bitterness, hostilities and hatred. Truly, this man's anger did not work the righteousness of God. Moreover, Esau was not a man of understanding, of wisdom or of knowledge with or about the spiritual things of God. Consequently, he had no regard for the blessings of Abraham. *(cf. Gen. 25:25, 34, 26:34, 27:1, 30, 33:49, 36:1; Rom. 9:13; Heb. 11:20, 12:16)*

An Underlying Current

Perhaps, no two Bible characters represent more fully the conflict between carnality and righteousness as do these twins, Jacob and Esau. The fact that Jacob supposedly cheated Esau of his birthright in *Genesis 27*, serves as the flashpoint for the underlying current of bitterness, hatred and strife between two brothers and a family of nations! The Prophet, Obediah, records four hostilities of the Edomites, who were the descendants of Esau in the following verses:

Obadiah 1:10-15 AMP
*"For **the violence you did against your brother Jacob**, shame shall cover you, and you shall be cut off forever. **On the day that you stood aloof** [from your brother Jacob] **on the day that strangers took captive his forces and carried off his wealth**, and foreigners entered into his gates and cast lots for Jerusalem-you were even as one of them. But **you should not have gloated over your brother's day, the day when his misfortune came and he was made a stranger;** you should not have rejoiced over the sons of Judah **in the day of their ruin; you should not have spoken arrogantly** in the day of their distress. You should not have entered*

the gate of My people in the day of their calamity and ruin; yes, ***you should not have looked [with delight] on their misery in the day of their calamity and ruin,*** *and not have reached after their army and their possessions in the day of their calamity and ruin. And* ***you should not have stood at the crossway to cut off those of Judah who escaped, neither should you have delivered up those [of Judah] who remained in the day of distress.*** *For the day of the Lord is near upon all nations. As you have done, it shall be done to you; your dealings will return upon your head."*

Specifically, the four hostilities which Esau committed against Jacob and his descendants are as follows:
- 1. He stood aloof, indifferent and unconcerned when Jacob was taken captive.
- 2. Esau gloated over Jacob's adversity and eventual ruin.
- 3. Esau spoke arrogantly about and against Jacob in the day of his distress.
- 4. Esau and his descendants apparently stood in ambush to cut off the escape route of all those who remained in Judah in the day of their distress. Commentaries state that Jacob had issues of his own, as we all have, but I would like to add the following postulation:

A Lifestyle of Carnality

Esau's carnal character was evident with his fleshly pursuits and self indulgent priorities for the here and now! These carnal tendencies were his short comings and as such, were his character flaws noted of God. I submit that Almighty God was not about to authorize Esau or any of his descendants to ascend to the throne of David, based upon such a lifestyle of carnality! The reason also being that Esau had no regard or respect for the blessings of Abraham which would have been his birthright, as the eldest of the two. Although God is no respecter of persons, He does show special regard to those who do respect their inheritance! *(cf. Acts 10:34-35)*

Esau had already married at least two Canaanite women, who were daughters of two great lords among the Canaanite people whose names were Helen and Esebon. As husband to these prominent women, Esau obtained authority and prestige, pretending to be something other than who he was. Although he was 40 years of age, Esau never had the blessings of his parents, because his marriages encumbered his own people with an unholy alliance and covenanted them to a godless nation.

What's In Your Wallet?

Capital One is a lending institution. Their advertised punch line is "What's in your wallet?" Well, the issues of one's life represents their true heart, just as a wallet laden with Credit Cards represents impulsiveness! People are known by and through their conduct and behavior. We are also known by the purposes and intents of our heart by Almighty God, for He knows the hearts of all men. *(cf. 1 Sam. 16:7; Acts 1:24, 15:8)* Since, Esau exposed his true, carnal self to God, by way of the true purposes and intents of his character, he could not possibly know that he alone was his own adversary. I believe that Esau would have only squandered his birthright during his life, thus frustrating the intents and purposes of God and that of a future nation. After all, why should one carnally minded man be allowed to ruin or hinder God's salvation plan?

Esau had no understanding of spiritual things, for the things of God were foolishness to him. And since repentance is a spiritual gift of God, Scriptures state that he had no place of repentance, even though he sought for it with tears after the fact. *(cf. Heb. 12:17) Micah 1:16* states in part, "to make thee bald...enlarge thy baldness." Baldness is an act of repentance and based upon Esau's character, he definitely needed a shave! Whereas, the hair on his body portrayed extreme carnality, baldness represents true godly repentance!

Obadiah 1:8b
"...there shall not be any remaining of the house of Esau."

Like Achin in Joshua chapter seven, Esau's posterity would be destroyed. **Truth #223: A lifestyle of repentance denotes that the saint possesses an understanding of the knowledge of salvation and that he teach repentance to his posterity!** Since repentance is a spiritual thing, it is essential that the saints of God understand it and appreciate their inheritance. Without this knowledge of salvation, carnality rises to fill the void of one's unregenerate soul. The end of which is death, eternal!

Respect Your Inheritance

Acts 11:18 teaches that repentance was granted as a gift to the gentiles unto real life after resurrection, which speaks of salvation! *Esau relinquished his gift not when Jacob "cheated" him out of his birthright, but when he deprived himself of his inheritance through his carnal living and his self indulgent priorities, beforehand.*

The Elder to Serve the Younger

In *Genesis 25:22-23* God told Rebekah, Esau's mother, that the elder would serve the younger, because God knew ahead of time that Esau would be unsuitable for His plan of the ages. *The point is that we cheat ourselves of our birthright, as long as we choose to live a carnal life.* The adverse events of our lives often are reflections of this.

A Savior to Judge

Obediah 1:21
"And saviors shall come... to judge..."

Left to ourselves, man's wickedness will become his rule. It is for this reason that mankind needs a savior to judge. God has sent His prophets to address the corruption of fallen humanity throughout the centuries. Their message was the same, in that they preached righteousness and judgment. Obadiah, a prophet of God, was no different. Many Messianic Prophecies spoke of Jesus Christ, the Lamb of God, who would one day die for the sins of humanity. Since then, we are left with God's eternal Word of life from which man was/is to benefit by. Man is to judge the mountain of his carnality himself in light of Scripture. If he chooses not to, then he shall be judged by the mountain of God's righteousness from whom the heavens and the earth fled away. *(cf. Dan.7:9-10; Rev. 20:11-15)* **Truth #224: Through a lifestyle of repentance, a contrite spirit and broken and penitential heart will attract God's favor; and His regard shall be upon that saint whose heart is broken down with sorrow for the ascent of his carnality, and who is truly humble and thoroughly penitent before the Lord his God!** *(cf. Ps. 34:10, 18, 51:17; Is. 57:15; 66:2)*

Chapter 32

Repentance in the Book of Jonah

The Pursuit is On

The pursuit is on! Like a jack rabbit that flees for its life or the motorist who evades arrest by the police, Jonah was a man who also ran! Would to God that the Body of Christ would stop their running! God had commanded Jonah to cry against the great city of Nineveh *(cf. Jon. 1:2)* The fact that Jonah initially evaded this command, leaves me to believe that Jonah had some preconceived notion [resentment] against the Assyrians, which he harbored within his heart. This resentment, possibly based upon a traumatic memory of atrocities, caused Jonah to flee Tarshish and from the presence of the Lord God. Jonah basically choked up on the mandate of God, just as so many in the church today, who choke up at the word of truth presented them. Due to his Lie Based Thinking, Jonah could not receive more of God's truth, because these resentments had occupied certain compartments within the carnality of his unrenewed mind and his unregenerate soul.

Before anyone is able to receive more of God, they first must rid themselves of the junk within their souls and I'm not talking about a trained behavior (pain management) or a conditioned conduct. After all, even a drunk driver can perform the field sobriety tests (FSTs) rather well, despite his inebriation. Just because you may not do the bar scene, play the field, or sow your oats, does not mean too say that you have eliminated the deepest recesses of your heart [character] or your mind of its haunts that may date back years in your life.

The Hazards of a Pursuit

Any pursuit has been dangerous for me as a California Highway Patrol Officer. Not only was my life in peril, the state property to which I was assigned to was also jeopardized and the lives and property of others in harm's way, but also the driver of the fleeing vehicle I was pursuing. Oh, the thoughts that flooded my mind during each pursuit; the policies, rules, regulations, safety factors, final out come considerations, not to mention the adrenalin rush. No doubt the fleeing suspect also experienced the work ethic involved in the pursuit, but his knowledge of specifics was lacking, therefore he possessed no understanding of his actions. Ninety-nine percent of the time the fleeing suspect was apprehended, primarily because he could not outrun the radio or evade the helicopter. In like manner, it is down right difficult, dangerous and dumb to think that we can out run or out maneuver God!

In *Jonah 1:1-17*, we read of the peril Jonah had become to the life, limb and property of others while out at sea. The seaman who were the crew to the ship, considered Jonah to be the source of their dread. The threat of eminent peril was upon them! Their adrenalin was pumping and great anxiety and fear came upon them, due to the raging sea. In times of desperation, no one ever really knows what they would do or how they would react to overwhelming odds. These mariners eventually threw Jonah overboard where upon God had a great fish, at the ready, to swallow him whole. Once over board, instantly the storm-tossed sea became quiet and the vessel and crew were safe. (Note: This event gave rise to the phrase that any person who brings bad luck is said to be a Jonah.)

A Whale of a Time

Jonah 1:17

"Now the Lord had prepared and appointed a great fish to swallow up Jonah. And Jonah was in the belly of the fish three days and three nights."

God had prepared a great fish to swallow Jonah. In Hebrew, the word, *swallow* means, "to cover, to destroy, to consume, to tolerate, to take in, to recant, make the most of it, make the best of it, grin and bear it, take it on the chin, etc." The great fish did in fact swallow Jonah and this suggests to us just how much God Almighty has tolerated our flight! However, in *Acts 17:30-31* we read, "And the times of this ignorance, God winked at: but now commandeth all men everywhere to repent: Because he hath appointed a day of judgment in the which he shall judge the world in righteousness by that man whom he hath ordained…"

God's wink towards man's carnality is not a flicker of his approval! He is not saying, "That's my boy!" Rather, it is more a grimace of His despair, because God knows that it is not in the heart of man to direct his own steps, even though we think we can. I mean, just how long would you put up with the foolishness of another? Not for long! Society might tolerate lawlessness and stupidity for a while, but such negative intrusions into our culture and into our minds ends up polluting both.

Living at peace with all men, as much as is possible, does not mean that we must be victimized by the hostilities or the mobocracy of others. Look at Israel today and their terrorists attacks! The United States winks at Israel's response through diplomacy; but should another terrorist attack on American shores occur, just see how fast and decisively we respond to this anarchy.

This Fish Represents Bondage and Bondage has Depth
Jonah 2:1-3

"Then Jonah prayed to the Lord his God from the fish's belly, And said, I cried out of my distress to the Lord, and He heard me; out of the belly of Sheol cried I, and you heard my voice. For You have cast me into the deep, into the heart of the seas, and the floods surrounded me; all Your waves and Your billows passed over me."

Jonah acknowledged that God had cast him into the deep. Notice that he did not blame God for his flight. There is a difference! When we blame another, we shirk from our responsibility, thereby making another accountable for our mistakes. When we make excuses or reinforce existing defensive masquerades, we do so just to protect the carnal indulgence of our selfishness! However, when the truth is acknowledged, then we agree with the truth, no matter how deep it cuts. **Truth #225: Through a lifestyle of repentance, the saint of God is vomited from his deep bondage, because he has acknowledged the truth!** At such depths, true repentance soothes the heart and contributes to the renewing of the mind. Though we still may smell like fish, our outward appearance is the filth of worldliness yet to be cleaned up. Come to think of it, it is a biological fact, that any solid consumed, would soon be bleached white by the digestive juices of our digestive system. Can you imagine Jonah's appearance when he was vomited, having spent three days and nights inside the belly of this whale? I do believe that Jonah's appearance would make an albino look tanned! **Truth #226: Through a lifestyle of repentance, the saint protects the color of his heart's complexion, because repentance maintains his godly disposition!**

It's been said, "Higher levels, bigger devils." Well, I wish to add this adage: Deeper levels, smaller devils and fewer imps! The blessings of God extend even to the depths of that which lies in the bedrock of our carnality, to rid it from our conscience thereby freeing us to develop a godly character. It's like the strata of sedimentary earth in which geographers are able to investigate earth's history, by examining the soil deposits which appear as strata lines stacked or piled one on top of another such as may be found in the Grand Canyon and may be observed by any tourist. As pertaining to carnality, these strata lines consist of the layers of refuse, piled high over time, and are the fashions of carnal men and society as a whole. I now refer you to figure 1 on page 436, and for the rest of this topic about mountains, please continue to examine figure 1.

The Roots of the Mountains

Jonah 2:3
"And said, I cried out of my distress to the Lord, and He heard me; out of the belly of Sheol cried I, and You heard my voice."

It may be said that Jonah's environment was altogether contrary towards him. Often, circumstances in life rage against each of us, for nobody is spared. Like sparks and embers that fly wildly into the air above a raging fire, these circumstances can set on fire the chain of events in one's life. It is in such times that we find ourselves completely out of control and there seems to be no end in sight. Like Jonah, we must cry out to God, but unlike Jonah, we must never consider God only in times of crisis. Crisis Christians refuse to get to the root of the problem and seek only a band-aid God, while the truly penitent seek His righteousness. This great fish plummeted into the sounding depths and headed for the roots [bottoms] of the mountains of the earth! The bars of the earth were all about Jonah as a cage. *(cf. 2:6)* Such dungeons of imprisonment incarcerates people potentially for their entire lives! When the saint allows himself to delve deep into the murky depths of his soul, these bars of iniquitous thoughts (lies/preceptions) reveal themselves to be the precepts of men, the fashions of worldliness and the piles of refuse upon which he has built his life.

So let me ask you, Just what are the mountains in your life? To answer this, let's consider the geographic land feature of any mountain range. Geographically, a mountain is a large land mass, that extends at least one thousand feet above *sea level*. I emphasize sea level, because planet earth is nearly three-fourths covered by water. Therefore, this common *rule* has become the determining factor, internationally. All other land masses below sea level are not generally considered, because they are out of sight. Each land mass [continent] is not just a floatation device, as if tethered to a fixed object! Every land mass is actually a plateau or a mountain peak! Any encyclopedic cross section of the ocean would show this. Furthermore, the mountain ranges that are above sea level, though they may be thousands of feet high, are for the most part extensions or protrusions of the land mass below sea level. In fact, the roots of the mountains extend some seven miles plus down! The Marianas Trench, for example, is over thirty-eight thousand feet deep. The world's highest mountain peak is Mount Everest in the Himalayas, located on the border of Nepal and Tibet. It is 29, 028 feet tall! That's nearly five and one half miles high! So from the highest elevation to the deepest, sounding depth there exist an approximate twelve and a half mile to a thirteen mile distance! So when you think of it, all of humanity are mountain top dwellers and there is a lot of room for error and improvement.

Three Types of Mountains

Both figuratively and literally, the Bible addresses three types of mountains. They are 1. The actual large land mass that extends thousands of feet above sea level. 2. The phantom mountains of temptation or circumstance in our present life. 3. The phantom mountains of our past life, upon which you and I have built our lives upon. In one sense, the Scriptures address the actual bedrock of terra firma, and in another sense they liken the foundations of the earth to be that of man's fundamental existence with his values or lack thereof, traditions, cultural differences, etc. *(cf. Rom. 15:12; Eph. 2:20; Heb. 6:1)* Some examples of this would be an idea or concept which bands people together such as our success, or our poverty, space exploration, wealth, education, denominations, ethnic or racial distinctions, morality or lack thereof, politics, and the like. But on a very heart level, what do these societal influences and cultural points of interest have to do with me or you, as an individual? Scripture provides an answer in *Matthew 21*.

Matthew 21:21-22
"...if ye have faith and doubt not, ye shall not only do this which is done to the fig tree, but also if ye shall say unto this mountain, be thou removed and be thou cast into the sea, it shall be done. All things whatsoever ye shall ask in prayer, believing, ye shall receive."

What mountain was Jesus referring to? Was He referring to the existing mountain beneath His feet or was He addressing the phantom trials and tribulations in life? Did He address the problems or impediments of daily life? Or is he providing a clue to that which is so deep, so imbedded in our past that we have been stumped and bewildered by it time and time again in our present? I believe that Jesus Christ was addressing all these in figurative terms, specifically those phantom mountain ranges which exist within the mind and their relationship with them in the subconscious realm and of our character. In effect, Jesus used an actual mountain, which the people of His day were familiar with, to illustrate a spiritual truth about the other two figurative types, which I will now address.

The Bible teaches that the heart knows its own bitterness and that there is a root of bitterness which exists within every man. *(cf. Prov. 14:10; Heb. 12:14-15)* So what then are these bitter roots and how were they planted and how have they grown? Who planted these roots [feelings] and why?

These are eternal questions, which every person should ponder for him or herself if he/she ever expects to mature. I am speaking of a psychological disposition, that has taken its root sometime in our past as growing from childhood to adulthood. Personally, I have cried out to God about my failures, my carnal tendencies, and my mental dispositions, only to fail time and again. **Truth #227: Since these twisted roots took their shape and were planted into my soul by events and situations and seasons of circumstance, so too must they be uprooted by events and seasons of circumstance that are just as forceful and deep reaching, thereby cancelling out the negative with a positive!** Yes, a confrontation with these phantom mountain ranges must occur if ever we expect to overcome the negative tendencies of carnality. Since this is a reasonable postulation, then it is also a reasonable supposition of spiritual truth.

Jesus Christ was born to die. He was beaten, humiliated, tortured, and died for the sins of the world. He gave his life, knowing what it would take. The crucifixion was brutal, ugly and a harsh death sentence. It was however, just the event necessary and of this magnitude of suffering, that cancelled out the brutality of sin and the ugliness and harshness of carnality! Almighty God provided in place of sin His mercy, grace, love and truth through Jesus Christ, the Light of God's Word of truth who dwelt among us. Since Jesus Christ suffered on the cross and now that he is risen, I am, you are and every person that has ever lived, has had at our finger tips the provisions needed to overcome the shackles of mountain influences! I say at our finger tips, because He has been and is just a praying phone call away. His phone number is 1 (333) *Jer. 33:3* and His emergency number is *Psalm 91:1*.

Jeremiah 33:3
"Call unto me and I will answer you and tell you great and mighty things which thou knowest not of."

Psalm 91:1 AMP
"He who dwells in the secret place of the Most High shall re-

main stable and fixed under the shadow of the Almighty [Whose power no foe can withstand]."

All this was accomplished so that each saint may possess and learn to use the essential mountain climbing equipment to overcome and reach the summit of the mountains in the realm of his carnality and the soulical elements of his being. So what are these phantom mountains? In order to answer this, I must first explain what constitutes the triunity of a man as defined in Scripture. Briefly stated, any man is first a spirit who lives in a physical body and who has a soul. Therefore...

- 1. Man is a spirit.

Genesis 1:26

"Let us make man in our image, after our likeness and let him have dominion..." Man is a spirit first; he was created by God who is Spirit. (cf. John 4:24)

- 2. Man has a soul, which consists of a mind, will and emotions. Together these become the elements of his character or personality. Man's soul is the combination of spirit and flesh. The following verse further validates this postulation.

1 Thessalonians 5:23

*"Now may the God of peace, himself sanctify you **wholly**, that your **spirit, soul** and **body** be preserved complete without blame at the coming of our Lord, Jesus Christ."* (emphasis mine)

- 3. Man has a body.

Genesis 2:7

"And the Lord God formed man of the dust of the ground and breathed into his nostrils the breath of life, and man became a living soul."

Our soul consists of our mind (intellect, conscience, subconscience, reasoning faculties), emotions and the will. Together they make up our character. It is the essence of who we are as living beings. Notice, that God did not say that man would become a living flesh. But he did say that man would become a living soul. *Since we are living souls, God encourages each of us to live in the spirit, but Satan influences us to live according to the flesh.* Our soul then is the battlefield, in which an eternal war rages. Now our soul comprises of all the elements of who we are individually. Since our mind is neutral and is an element of the soul, it becomes the primary target of carnal and spiritual devices. When our soul is attacked by phantom mountain influences, we are wounded internally. Our personalities, our thoughts and perceptions are then affected in one way or degree or another. Many times, when these injuries occur, mountains of refuse take root.

Now to answer the initial question, What are these mountains? They are the piles of refuse that are left behind by the carnal influences of unregenerate men, who have seized the opportunity to victimize you and I. These piles of refuse go unnoticed and are often built upon throughout the generations and eventually, may become generational curses all because of carnal men defrauding another. Society evinces this, when you stop and consider the utter mess in which we live, with all the psycho-babble that exists in any individual, family, community or nation; and within each of these, there are piles of refuse! They may include incest, adultery, spouse abuse, child molestation, felony assault and battery, alcoholism, ignorance, condemnation and timidity. Just to name a few.

What are the piles of refuse in your life? It will take courage to confront them and strength of heart to surmount them. But once encountered and exposed, Almighty God will promote you as you step through the thresholds that have long since bound you. The choice is yours. Life is an adventure; it's not just an existence! Whereas, your perspective of life, of others or of yourself may be low currently, with your hope in God and the help found in His word, you will soon find yourself standing on the summit of the mountains of His righteousness, with all the refuse under your feet. You will then view life from the vista of God's grace and love just for you, because you looked unto the mountain of God from whence cometh your help!

Isaiah 14:25 AMP
"That I will break the Assyrian in my land, and upon My mountains I will tread him under foot. Then shall the [Assyrian] yoke depart from [the people of Judah], and his burden depart from their shoulders."

Psalm 36:6
"Your righteousness is like the mountains of God, Your judgments are like the great deep, O Lord, You preserve man and beast."

Isaiah 2:1-3 AMP
"The word which Isaiah son of Amoz saw [revealed] concerning Judah and Jerusalem. It shall come to pass in the latter days that the mountain of the Lord's house shall be [firmly] established as the highest of the mountains and shall be exalted above the hills, and all nations shall flow to it. And many people shall come and say, Come, let us go up to the mountain of the Lord, to the house of Jacob, that He may teach us His ways and that we may walk in His paths. For out of Zion shall go forth the law and instruction, and the word of the Lord from Jerusalem."

Like some countries whose borders are the boundaries established by mountain ranges around and about them similarly, for the victim, the piles of refuse in his life are safety zones which provide protection from external forces. The generational curses and the emotional hang ups arise from the bedrock of deep rooted foundations. These foundations are the unseen and unknown elements caused by influential others in our past who have had a major impact on our over all development, whether good or bad. These exist, because our soul is passive and is affected by whatever motivation is placed in it. These also include the societal influences of our carnal tendencies in all areas of conduct and behavior.

Therefore, foundational roots are the chains of bondage that have entangled themselves in the unregenerate vestiges of the soul, specifically the faculties of our intellect, and subconscious.

Matthew 13:35
"...I will open my mouth in parables; I will utter things which have been kept secret from the foundation of the world."

Hebrews 1:10
"And, thou O Lord, in the beginning hast laid the foundation of the earth; and the heavens are the work of thine hands."

Romans 15:20
"Yea, so have I strived to preach the gospel, not where Christ was named, lest I should build upon another man's foundation."

Luke 3:3-6
"And he came into all the country about Jordan, preaching the baptism of repentance for the remission of sins; as it is written in the book of words of Esaias the prophet saying, The voice of one crying in the wilderness, prepare ye the way of the Lord, make his paths straight. Every valley shall be filled and every mountain and hill shall be brought low; and the crooked shall be made straight, and the rough ways shall be made smooth."

Job 28:9
"He puts his hand upon the rock, he over turns the mountains by the roots."

Matthew 3:10
"...the axe is laid at the roots." Incidently, the word root means, "deep, bottom, heel."

Job 19:28
"But ye should say, Why persecute ye him, seeing the root of the matter is found in him." (cf. Job 14:18)

Deuteronomy 29:29
"The secret things belong unto the Lord our God: but those things which are revealed belong unto us and to our children forever, that we may do all the works of the law."

Deuteronomy 30:3
"That then the Lord thy God will turn thy captivity, and have compassion upon thee, and will return and gather thee from all the nations, whither the Lord thy God hath scattered thee."

Job 39:8
"The range of the mountains is His pasture, and he searches after every green thing."

Psalm 46:1-3
"God is our refuge and our strength, a very present help in the time of need. Therefore, will not we fear, though the earth be removed, and though the mountains be carried into the midst of the sea; though the waters thereof roar and be troubled and though the mountains shake with the swelling thereof..."

Psalm 50:11
"I know all the fowls of the mountains, and the wild beasts of the field are mine."

Jeremiah 1:10
"...to root out, and to pull down, and to destroy, and to throw down, to build and to plant."

Deuteronomy 32:22
"For a fire is kindled in mine anger, and shall burn unto the lowest hell and shall consume the earth with her increase, and set on fire the foundations of the mountains."

Mountain of Righteousness to Arise Above the Mountain of Carnality

Psalm 35:23
"Arouse yourself, awake to the justice due me, even to my cause, my God and my Lord!" (cf. 1 Cor. 15:34)

Psalm 36:6
"Your righteousness is like the mountains of God, Your judgments are like the great deep..." (cf. Ps. 107:24; 1 Cor. 2:10)

Isaiah 2:2 AMP
"It shall come to pass in the latter days that **the mountain of the Lord's house** shall be [firmly] established as **the highest of the mountains** and shall be **exalted above the hills**, and all nations shall flow to it." (emphasis mine)

When a man arouses himself to justice which is due him, he also awakens to righteousness towards him, for in righteousness he obtains the knowledge of God. *(cf. 1 Cor. 15:34)* This knowledge is the means by which he shall overcome the piles of refuse within his soul. Therefore, when God's righteousness is established within the soul, then the saint becomes as a mountain of God, because he has received of God the judgment [gift of repentance] and is now able to surmount the phantom mountain ranges of carnality, that has for so long hemmed him in! In effect, the saint progressively grows up in the knowledge of God, through faith in Christ. And as he does so, the critical mass of his faith empowers the saint to remove these piles of refuse from his life. Here is a faith ditty from one of my earlier books, entitled 'The Aspects of the Audacity of Faith'.

Critical mass is the least amount of fissile material needed to sustain a nuclear reaction under a given set of conditions. Critical mass is also the minimum amount or number required for something to happen or begin. Therefore, mountain moving faith is faith that has been concentrated, intensified and containerized for the optimum result!

The Rejection of Bondage

Like castor oil that is swallowed, this great fish regurgitated Jonah! Jonah's experience outside and inside the whale compelled his break through! Deep repentance enables us to experience breakthroughs as well. Whenever someone endures a surgical operation such as an organ transplant, without the proper medication, there's a good chance that the transplanted organ may be rejected by the recipient body. Medication is provided to offset this biological rejection. Again, whenever a rose bush is transplanted, the earth usually rejects the bush, and so potting soil is provided to condition the earth to accept the bush. **Truth #228: Through a lifestyle of repentance, any bondage shall vomit the saint, because he allowed himself to feel a pain which God wanted him to feel; and the Word of God is as the potting soil, by which the saint has transplant-**

ed his heart in righteousness! After all, the only other option is total rejection from God. Had Jonah not reconsidered, I believe that God would have allowed that whale to totally consume him as fish food.

In summary, the reason that we are rejected from the source of our bondage is because the bondage does not want to die. So we must die to it! Any bondage exists due to the piles of refuse from which our worldly life is built. They are the phantom mountain ranges [the fashions of men] which God expects His saints to overcome. **Truth #229: Moreover, just as any mountain climber would vomit, due to the extreme altitudes he has exposed himself too; likewise, a lifestyle of repentance will cause the saint to be vomited and like any regurgitation, it hurts!** Through a lifestyle of repentance, we escape the wrath of God because we have been regurgitated from our bondage! (cf. Rev. 2:5, 21:7-8)

Blood Boiling Mad

I am a big teddy bear. You don't believe me? It takes a lot to get me to the point of anger. Usually, I get disgusted and frustrated, but seldom do I really become enraged. However, there are times when my blood boils instantly. On the one hand, I am as a pot of water on a real slow simmer. Then on the other, I can flare up due to oppressive circumstances that tend to pull me back into old patterns of thinking and living. Where the first might buffet me due to the external activities about me, the other attacks the internal treasures of my heart, such as my dignity and my integrity. *A lifestyle of repentance therefore, is a very vital tool or weapon to safe guard my heart. Notice, I used the word vital, because repentance applies to the vital organ which is my heart [character]. Just as there are heart attacks physically, likewise, there are heart attacks spiritually. (cf. Zeph. 2:1-3)*

We Must Guard Ourselves Against the Gourds of Life
Jonah 4:1-3 AMP

"But it displeased Jonah exceedingly and he was very angry. And he prayed to the Lord and said, I pray You, O Lord, is not this just what I said when I was in my country? That is why I fled to Tarshish, for I knew that You are a gracious God and merciful, slow to anger and of great kindness, and [when sinners turn to You and meet Your conditions] You revoke the [sentence of] evil against them. Therefore now, O Lord, I beseech You, take my life from me, for it is better for me to die than to live."

Chapter 4 begins with a very angry prophet. Rather than obey God, Jonah would rather die and all because of a bondage. Whether He was serious about this or whether he was attempting to manipulate God, I don't know. Have you ever felt that way? I believe you have. We all have encountered people who have tried to control our lives with manipulative tactics, promises and threats. Isn't it amazing how often, we allow a thing to have dominion over our life!

In verses 6-11 of chapter 4, we read that God created a gourd to shield a rebellious prophet from the scorching heat of the desert sun. Sometime during the night, God caused a cut worm to spoil this gourd. As Jonah slept, God prepared to teach His bitter prophet an object lesson. Since God knows the hearts of men, He wanted to expose a bondage within the deepest recesses of Jonah's carnality. Having no protection from the sun, Jonah became very wroth again over the loss of this gourd. In other words, the gourd and Jonah's selfishness had the first priority over the one hundred twenty thousand lives of the inhabitants of Nineveh and the herds of innocent cattle! Because we live in a material society or earth environment, we must guard ourselves against the gourds of life. **Truth #230: Through a lifestyle of repentance, we get our priorities straight in that we place the** value of souls above the material things in our life. In doing so, the saint guards himself against the gourds in his life!

In closing, the experiences which Jonah had greatly influenced the message of repentance. As of this date September 15, 2001, and on the heals of the terrorist attacks on American soil, I sense that Americans have realized the truth of God's displeasure with our improprieties, because we have placed a value and therefore a priority on the material thing over people and our relationship with Almighty God! As we shall see in the book of Haggai, the people of his day placed a value and a priority on the material thing, specifically their individual houses with their ceiled roofed dwellings and neglected the house of God. **Truth #231: Through a lifestyle of repentance, the saint considers his ways, thereby establishing the word of God's righteousness in his own heart!**

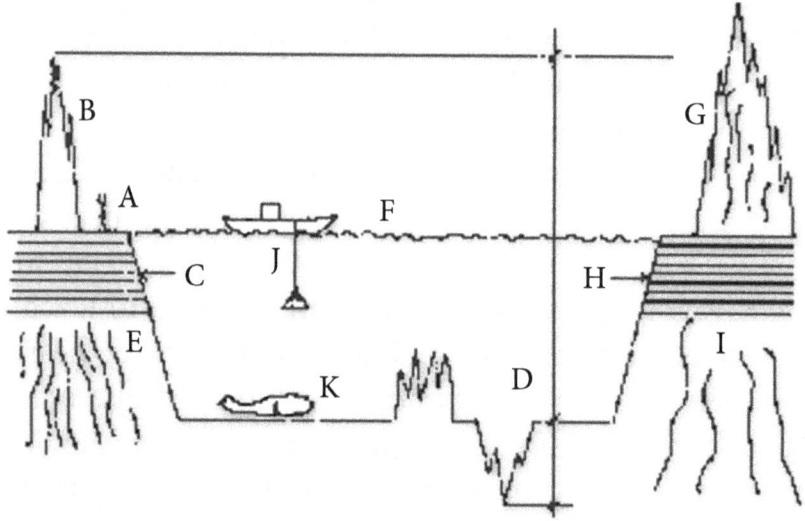

A. Man, fettered to his Carnality
B. Mountain of Carnality
C. Strata Lines of Carnality
D. Piles of Refuse
E. Roots of the Mountains

F. Waters of Regeneration
G. Mountains of Righteousness
H. Strata Lines of Fruit of the Spirit
I. Rooted and Grounded in Righteousness
J. Gospel Ship with Line of Judgment and Anchor of Righteousness
K. Great Fish of God's Mercy and Uncompromised Call

Notes:

Chapter 33
Repentance in the Book of Micah

Micah 1:13
"Bind the chariot to the swift steed, O lady of Lachish: you were the beginning of sin to the Daughter of Zion, for the transgressions of Israel were found in you."

The graven images which the leadership moved Israel to worship were the transgressions of Jacob. (1:5) In verse 13, we read, "...she is the beginning of sin to the Daughter of Zion;..." It seems that these corrupt political and spiritual leaders goaded the people to idol worship, so as to conceal there true idols of greed, oppression and theft and all at the expense of the people whom they lorded over!

The First to be Punished

There are those saboteurs, who worm their way into congregations, assemblies, communities and nations covertly, as sleeper agents of hell. Their cunning clandestine disguises enables them to intermingle into a host populace, to be concealed or absorbed therein. In deed, they are leeches upon an unsuspecting prey! I'm thinking of the saboteur A'chin, who in Joshua chapter seven, took of the accursed thing and buried it in his tent with all his stuff. A'chin, who initially was successful in avoiding detection, was found guilty of sabotage, for his transgression caused thirty-six warriors to die just so he could gloat over his selfishness! However, A'chin failed to realize that Almighty God knew his address and literally read his mail! His sin of theft and idolatry destroyed himself, his family as well as the thirty-six brave warriors who were killed in battle, due to his sin. My point is, the ringleader who introduces sin shall be the first to be punished, and that more severely!

Make Thee Bald

Micah 1:16 AMP

"Make yourself bald in mourning and cut off your hair for the children of your delight; enlarge your baldness as the eagle, for [your children] shall be carried from you into exile."

▶ **True to Life:** The national bird of the United States of America, whose head and neck is covered with white feathers, although not bald, is known as the American Bald Eagle. A cancer patient may temporarily loose his/her hair, due to chemotherapy treatments, leaving him/her completely bald. Tires, worn of their tread, are called bald tires and are generally considered a violation of the vehicle code. Baldness is also a common feature of an older man's appearance, although it may occur with younger men, too. I was a recruit at the United States Marines Corps Recruit Depot in Parris Island in the summer of 1970. As a recruit, I was promptly deprived of my mop [hair]. And years later, as a Drill Instructor myself, I had the distinct pleasure of watching my herd lose theirs! Truly, what goes around, comes around!

▶ **True to Scripture:** The Prophet, Elisha was bald headed. *(cf. 2 Kgs. 2:23)* Samson was shaved bald by Delila. *(cf. Judg. 16:17)* In chapter fourteen of Leviticus, those who had contracted leprosy were shaved bald of all their hair. The people of Moab mourned in baldness and covered themselves and their houses with sackcloth! *(cf. Is. 15:2-3; Jer. 48:36-40)* Even the mariners shaved themselves bald, as they mourned in sackcloth at the destruction of Tyre. *(cf. Ezek. 27:29-32)* But the question I have is this, Why did Micah speak of an eagle that molts and not an animal that sheds?

Balderdash

To the carnally minded man, spiritual truths are rejected because they are considered foolish by him. He does not welcome or accept them, because to him, spiritual truths are balderdash [nonsense]! There are many people within the halls of Christendom and Government who make the claim of their Christianity and yet to these, God's Word still remains as balderdash [nonsense]! Like Elisha, who was mocked for his baldness by the juveniles in *2 Kings 2:23*, and like Samson whose hair was shaved in *Judges 16:17*, the condition of their baldness was the item of interest.

The Balderdash of Repentance

▶ **True to Reason:** As pertaining to the recruit, baldness strips him of his civilian dignity as his sloppy head dress is rent even to the bone! Talk about shearing stress! Although his hair has been sheared, the follicle remains. In time, his hair reappears however, next time, the Marine wears his hair according to military regulations. A recruit's hair is also sheared for purposes of hygiene, and so it must be for the saint. Speaking for myself, my once youthful forehead has been enlarging it's acreage for many a year! Those hairs of my head eat a lot of lettuce! Baldness therefore, is a spiritual representation of repentance and it coincides with sackcloth. **Truth #232: Baldness portrays a lifestyle of repentance, for it is something that the saint must do to suppress the continual growth of his carnality!**

Although our hair grows again, we wear it in accordance to scriptural regulations. Furthermore, the slow, gradual and daily growth of hair symbolizes the persistent resurgence of carnality, which must be kept in check! A lifestyle of repentance enables us to do this.

Notes:

Chapter 34
Repentance in the Book of Nahum

An Antecedent to Destruction

The Book of Nahum presents a foreboding future for Nineveh, the ancient city of Iraq and it is believed by some scholars, that the book of Nahum was written as a sequel to the book of Jonah. As the Scriptures attest, the great city of Nineveh once repented in sackcloth and ashes, during the day of Jonah. However, approximately one hundred fifty years later, the people of this Assyrian city recanted their reverence for Almighty God through their backsliding into gross idolatry once again. Therefore, God raised another man, the Prophet Nahum, to address the wickedness of a rebellious people once more. As a response to Jonah's message, "Yet forty days, and Nineveh shall be over-thrown," the king and all the citizens of this city repented in sackcloth and ashes as an antecedent to their destruction! *(cf. Jon. 3:4-10)* **Truth #233: A lifestyle of repentance is the precedent that precedes righteous judgment, because man's premise of God's loving-kindness and mercy are the basis for His argument against man's carnality!** Now one hundred fifty years later, in this book of Nahum, we read of Nineveh's destruction, along with Judah and Israel, for their severe wickedness.

Similarly, on Tuesday morning, September 11th, 2001, America experienced a harbinger of God's displeasure of her own, the wake of which impacted every American, here and abroad! Then on Thursday, September 13, 2001, President Bush called this single day a *national day of remembrance* of all those who lost their lives caused by the violent catastrophe. *Where carnal man surmises that his silent tribute represents true repentance, the saint of God understands that, at the very least, a day of his atonement symbolizes his repentance as a condition of his contrite heart!* It's just my opinion therefore, that September 13th should have been a day for America's national repentance. **Truth #234: Like the rod that is used for the back of fools, so too is righteous judgment the utensil that is applied to the hearts of impenitent men!** *(cf. Prov. 10:13, 26:3)* The strength of any nation or its people resides in their compliance to the terms and conditions of Almighty God and America is not excluded!

Jonah 3:9 AMP
"Who can tell, God may turn and revoke His sentence against us [when we have met His terms], and turn away from His fierce anger so that we perish not."

Joel 2:13 AMP
"Rend your hearts and not your garments and return to the Lord, your God, for He is gracious and merciful, slow to anger, and abounding in loving-kindness; and He revokes His sentence of evil [when His conditions are met]."

Hebrews 12:9-11 AMP
"Moreover, we have had earthly fathers who disciplined us and we yielded [to them] and respected [them for training us]. Shall we not much more cheerfully submit to the Father of spirits and so [truly] live? For [our earthly fathers] disciplined us for only a short period of time and chastised us as seemed proper and good to them; but He disciplines us for our certain good, that we may become sharers in His own holiness. For the time being no discipline brings joy, but seems grievous and painful; but afterwards

it yields a peaceable fruit of righteousness to those who have been trained by it [a harvest of fruit which consists in righteousness-in conformity to God's will in purpose, thought, and action, resulting in right living and right standing with God]."

As of this writing, President Bush is contemplating war with Iraq. It's my prayer that history will repeat itself in that the leadership and citizens of both America and Iraq would once again adorn themselves with sackcloth and ashes as those works meet for repentance, from Presidents George Bush and Saddam Hussein down to the innocent cattle of each nation! *(cf. 2 Cor. 7:8-10)*

Notes:

Chapter 35
Repentance in the Book of Habakkuk

A Tale of Two Cities

Upon reading Habakkuk, I was reminded of the men who travailed in the streets of Jerusalem in the midst of all the abominations of their day. *(cf. Ezek. 9:4-6)* In Ezekiel, we learned of an impersonal, objective view of the repentance of these unidentified men. However, in Habakkuk, I find a more subjective and therefore personal perspective of the Prophet concerning Judah, some thirty-one years later. Let me explain. We read in Ezekiel, that God commanded the unidentified man with the ink horn to set a mark upon the foreheads of the unidentified men in travail. This mark spared these righteous men in the day of God's judgment. Well with Habakkuk, it is evident that this Prophet of God was a travailing man in his day and to his city, just like his predecessor, Jeremiah. Habakkuk was an eyewitness and as such, he was a reporter at "ground zero" in Judah. And from his perspective, as a citizen of a targeted city, he broadcasted the death and destruction all about him. He even expressed his feelings of dismay and foreboding within himself. The fact that Habakkuk lived through a city wide catastrophe, tells me that the people ignored his preaching of God's judgment and righteousness and not just his, but even that of the prophets before him!

America's Ground Zero

America had its own ground zero, when on Tuesday morning, September 11th 2001, the twin towers of the World Trade

Center were targeted and this nation trembled even to the bone! Of interest was the fact that each building that collapsed, bore the insignia of the WTC. All others buildings that did not display this insignia remained standing! From ground zero, eye-witness news reporters, filmed and broadcasted to the entire world the utter chaos and confusion caused by this calamity of immense proportions. Elsewhere around the country, personal interviews with "the man on the street" convinced the rest of America and the world of the stark terror and shear horror of this coordinated attack upon the economy and the psyche of every American.

That Which Begs the Question

Habakkuk knew of the oppressive and corrupt ways of his people and of their leadership. In spite of this, Habakkuk had to ask a question of God. "How can You, O Lord, allow another wicked nation to prosper at the expense of Your people and at the hands of a wicked nation who is more evil than us?" *(cf. Hab. 1:13)* Today, in light of September 11th, America has basically asked the same question. Why, have these evil people waged war against us, when they are more wicked than we? The witness to my heart is simply that America has forgotten that Almighty God looks upon the heart felt motivations of all men, for He alone knows that should impenitent humanity ever come to true repentance and depart from their wickedness, we would then understand that we are carnal. Only then will the external devices of wickedness cease.

Job 28:28
"And unto man he said, Behold, the fear of the Lord, that is wisdom; and to depart from evil is understanding." (cf. Prov. 3:7, 16:6, 17)

Matthew 7:22-23 AMP

"Many will say to Me on that day, Lord, Lord, have we not prophesied in Your name and driven out demons in Your name and done many mighty works in Your name? And then I will say to them openly (publicly) I never knew you: depart from Me, you who act wickedly [disregarding My commands]."

America's Wake Up Call

The alarm was set. At precisely 08:48 Tuesday morning on September 11th, 2001 it sounded, but a sleepy, fattened nation, like a herd of cattle, just rolled over stuffing her head under the pillows of contentment and passivity, regretting the alarm to awake. As people do, they preset a second alarm, usually ten to twenty minutes later to rouse them out of bed. At precisely 09:06, just eighteen minutes later, the second alarm sounded! America did in fact wake up to the reality that she was under a terrorist attack. But now there is a lull. It seems that America has once again wallowed back into a national selfishness, which is her social conscience, and has found herself more consumed with the material thing of playing catch up for all that was lost and the pursuit of pleasure; rather than come to repentance before a just and righteous God. *Because carnality is denied, self righteousness prevails! Therefore, since God's righteousness is ignored carnality continues to thrive!*

Judgment And Righteousness, Ignored

Like the people of Habakkuk's day, it was evident by Scripture that they too ignored the preaching of righteousness and judgment, just as America has done today. American society has once again chased hard after the material thing leaving God completely out of the picture. Although times and places may change, people who are left to themselves, really don't. **Truth #235: A lifestyle of repentance sets the standard upon the un-**

righteous, because the remnant of God are His preachers of righteousness to an unrighteous world, in and through their lifestyle of repentance!

Saviors of God

Obadiah 1:21
"And saviors shall come up on Mount Esau and the kingdom shall be the Lords."

Habakkuk was just one of the many saviors sent of God to judge [to set a standard of righteousness] before the impenitent people of God; but because they rejected God's standard bearer and his message, they would fall to the standard of the occupation of a hostile and corrupt nation worse than they! Today, in post 9/11 America, God's judgment and righteousness are still ignored! *Impenitent America will soon fall beneath the righteous standard of the unrighteous occupation of a hostile and corrupt Islamic insurgence.* We, who have adopted a lifestyle of repentance are to continue to preach by word and deeds, the message of judgment and righteousness, so that all should come to repentance, before it's too late! I emphasize should because repentance is an obligation, and a duty, which must become a desired expectation of each person. However, Scriptures tell us that most will not. *(cf. Mat. 7:13-14; 2 Pet. 3:9-11; Rev. 9:20-21)*

The Exalted State of Carnality

Obadiah 1:21 above reads in part, *"...to judge the Mount of Esau..."* This mount represents the exalted state of one's carnality. Although Satan has already been judged, his influence, that residue of sin, still resides within the soul. **Truth #236: A lifestyle of repentance is a lifelong forensic investigative process of self examination! The mounting evidence of carnality has heaped up as piles of refuse; as that mountain range of man's**

tradition, of his institutions and his denominationalism all of which have usurped the commandments of God throughout the generations! *Note: Forensic is defined as the speciality in application of scientific knowledge to legal matters, as in the investigative process of a crime. (Webster's)*

Notes:

Chapter 36
Repentance in the Book of Zephaniah

A Time for Repentance
Zephaniah 2:1-3 AMP
"Collect your thoughts, yes, unbend yourselves [in submission and see if there is no sense of shame and no consciousness of sin left in you]. O shameless nation [not desirous or desired]! **[The time for repentance is speeding by like chaff whirled before the wind!]** *Therefore consider, before God's decree brings forth [the curse upon you], before* **the time [to repent]** *is gone like the drifting chaff, before the fierce anger of the Lord comes upon you-yes, before the day of the wrath of the Lord comes upon you! Seek the Lord [inquire for Him, inquire of Him, and require Him as the foremost necessity of your life], all you humble of the land* **who have acted in compliance with His revealed will and have kept His commandments;** *seek righteousness, seek humility [inquire for them, require them as vital]. It may be you will be hidden in the day of the Lord's anger."* (emphasis mine)

Once again, a nation is exhorted to repent and to seek righteousness as a social conscience. In *Matthew 24:16*, it is written that those who are in Judea were to flee to the mountains. Yet, here in this passage, Scripture reads, "Collect yourselves together." Where the former says scatter, the latter says gather. Since there is a season, and a *time* for every matter or purpose under heaven, as Ecclesiastes chapter three specifies, then this also must include a season for repentance and a *time* to repent as noted in these text verses. As addressed previously, the purpose for divine judgment is to judge wickedness and the reason of judgment is that the saint would exact judgment against his own carnality. Moreover, as was also addressed in Deuteronomy, the purpose for repentance is to exhume the reason of it, namely iniquitous thoughts. But just when is the season of repentance? In light of this investigation, that season must be the entire life of a living soul. And the *time* to repent is now, for today is the day of salvation.

But speaking of *time*, let's consider for the *time* being, the *time* for repentance. In a previous chapter, I spoke of marking *time* as it relates to repentance and how the grape treader, in the vat and the military unit marching in place, got nowhere fast. In spite of this apparent waste of *time*, it should be evident that no *time* was wasted! The truth is that those who have adopted a lifestyle of repentance have not wasted any of their time of sojourn on this planet during the *time* of their living. Consequently then, a *time* to repent and the *time* for repentance are crucial *times* in one's life, for should a man pass his *time* away without giving himself the *time* of the day in which he lives, he shall be ignorant of his future *time* [his latter end] and shall experience another *time* to burn in the lake of fire reserved for the devil and his fallen angels, for without repentance, he literally kills *time*. Either way, after resurrection, everybody shall experience a *time* without end, because we are eternal spirit beings.

Often it is said how fast *time* passes by or how quickly *time* flies. Well these adages are very applicable to the *time* for repentance, which is speeding by like chaff that is whirled away in the wind. Just look at your own life and consider just how fast the last decade has flown by! Truly, man's existence on earth is as a shadow which appears for a very brief moment in *time* and then is vanished.

As Scripture indicates, a day with the Lord is equivalent to a thousand earth years and a thousand earth years are equal to a single day with the Lord. *(cf. 2 Pet. 3:8)* When you think of the twenty-four hour day and how swiftly it comes and goes, it should be no problem to expand your imagination to comprehend the significance of this *time* for repentance, before it's to late! As any prisoner who is paying his debt to society by doing *time*, likewise, Almighty God commands that humanity serve their *time* by doing repentance, for how else shall anyone become a prisoner of the Lord, Jesus Christ? *(cf. Rom. 11:32)* **Truth #237: The time for repentance is a time of refreshing, for the penitent saint seeks righteousness and because he does so, he shall be concealed in the day of God's wrath upon an unrighteous world, primarily because he won't be here!**

The Prophet Zephaniah was the great grandson, three times removed, to King Hezekiah. Since Zephaniah was of royal blood, God tasked Zephaniah to preach righteousness to the corrupt government of his day. In God's eyes, secular leadership is equal to spiritual leadership. Therefore, God will send prophets to speak to presidents, kings, emperors and potentates. This association is observed in every prophetic book. It is for this reason that government leadership at all levels, judge righteously, to love mercy and to walk humbly before Almighty God. *(cf. Mic. 6:8)*

The Cycle of Grace

In the movie, The Lion King, the circle of life was spoken of. Well, in *2 Chronicles 7:14*, we read that God shall heal the land. What the circle of life may be to the animal kingdom, God's cycle of grace is to the kingdom of man! Just as all things die and return to dust, man shall also return to powder, for this is the way of all the earth. Perhaps this is why Peter encourages each of us to grow in grace and knowledge, as the grace deposits made [by God into His saints] shall be the return of the dividends given! *(cf. 2 Pet. 3:18)* The cycle of grace shall resurrect those who are or have been saved by amazing grace through faith. *(cf. Eph. 2:8-9; 1 Pet. 1:7-9)* **Truth #238: Therefore, a lifestyle of repentance is as an emollient oil, which lubricates the wheel of the cycle of grace upon any land, nation or people!** Since humanity was fathered by God, in that Adam and Eve were created in His image, then it is reasonable to postulate that righteous humanity shall return once again to their heavenly Father, whose maker is God. Whereas, the unrighteous shall be transferred to the home of their choosing and be joined to their progenitor and their father of liars, whom they mimicked in their unrighteousness while on earth.

Chapter 37
Repentance in the Book of Haggai

The Lollygagging Church
Most people are quick to talk of events, past and present. Such mental preoccupations, whether factual or historical, rarely if ever, engage an urge for change. If we suppose that the knowledge of history alone could cause people to change from their carnality to righteousness, then history alone would also show that the people changed, could eventually relapse from righteousness back into their carnality, as did the Ninevites, one hundred fifty years after Jonah preached repentance to them. If anything, history supports the futility of man's attempts towards false peace in his self righteousness and his meager attempts of rehabilitation with his moral code of society, universal. I say false peace, because Scripture states that *the effect of righteousness will be peace, both internal and external and the result of righteousness will be quietness and confident trust forever, because God's people shall dwell in peaceable habitations, in safe dwellings and in quiet resting places. (cf. Is. 32:17-18)* **Truth #239: Therefore, what rehabilitation may be to an inmate's restoration, reconciliation is to the saint's transformation from his carnality to spiritual maturity!** *(cf. Heb. 12:8-11)*

Eighteen years had already come and gone since the Hebrews were set free of their Babylonian captivity. However, the building of the now discarded temple of God had laid in ruins for decades and its reconstruction was hindered by those hostile to its renovation; but also by the lollygagging people of God who seemingly gave in to them! Prior to this, the prophets of God were mocked and murdered and as a consequence upon the Hebrews, the Lord closed the prophetic vision in those days, because the Word of God had become scarce. This is also obvious when between the Old and New Testaments, Almighty God remained mute to the things of carnal men. The result of which allowed the inception of the many disciplines of secular philosophy to take root as a social conscience within the masses of carnal humanity. *(cf. 1 Sam. 3:1; Ps. 74:9)*

Ephesians 4:11-13 states in essence, that the prophet, among the other spiritual leadership gifts to the New Testament Church, exist for the perfection of the saints and the work of the ministry unto the edification of the Body of Christ, until we all come into the unity of faith. This unity reminds me of *Matthew 6:33* which denotes that we seek first the kingdom of God and His righteousness. **Truth #240: A lifestyle of repentance is a pursuit of righteousness, which produces peace; whereas a lollygagging church is symptomatic of a careless, spiritual refrain! Through repentance then, any carnal restraint is an effect of righteousness unto godliness and peace!**

The Dawdling Church

Dawdle means, "to waste time over trifles and frittering away time that makes for slow progress." (Webster's) Well it seems that for eighteen years, this was precisely what the Hebrews did. Today, there are many, who are doing the same thing! An unstructured day, displays a passive mind that is purposeless and unplanned. Such a lifestyle denotes a scarcity of discipline for ethics of work and a resultant life of despondency and despair. Literally, you are in a rut! Dawdling is taking the path of least resistance and allowed to continue, it erodes spiritual disciplines for godliness.

Therefore, **Truth #241: A lifestyle of repentance is necessary to counteract the passivity of one's carnality!** Otherwise, we merely exist as inanimate objects of creation, who are guilty of loitering about at the cross! The Hebrews never said that they would not reconstruct the temple. They just said, "Not yet!" They needed an external force to activate them. Like cattle that are prodded, people often need an outside agitation or boost to engage their creativity.

Carnal Bruising

Isaiah 53:5 AMP
"But He was wounded for our transgressions, He was bruised for our guilt and iniquities..."

I've heard it said, "You're cruising for a bruising!" Well, Almighty God sent His Son on a cruise to earth to be bruised on our behalf, because it takes a bruise to spiritually heal another bruise! Carnal bruising indicates mannerisms which are objective symptoms of an existing carnal tendency for self indulgence. Like dark paint that bleeds through a lighter color applied over it, such bruising bleeds into one's character. You could say that this carnality makes one a bleeding heart. Or like the injury of blood vessels or veinal capillaries beneath the skin, which testifies that a blunt force has occurred at that sight of injury. Carnal bruising is symptomatic of a wounding which has previously occurred to the soul, stunting and shunting maturation and spiritual disciplines. **Truth #242: Through a lifestyle of repentance, the righteous bruise which Jesus Christ received on our behalf, supplants the carnal bruise which Satan applied to the soul of man, as a brand of his usurpation against the authority of Almighty God!**

In the case with Haggai, the Hebrews were carnally "hoodwinked" into deceit. How about you? Have you been hoodwinked? Has some circumstance or season of events in your life pulled the wool over your eyes, blinding you to what the truth of God's Word has to say about you or about your particular situation? Or have you become a passive, inanimate object ? The word *passive* means, "a mind set that awaits for an external force to activate it." If this is you, then allow the word of God to be that external force which activates your soul for renewal and prods your regeneration.

Not Yet!

Haggai 1:2 AMP
"Thus says the Lord of hosts: These people say, The time is **not yet** come that the Lord's house should be rebuilt [although Cyrus had ordered it done eighteen years before]." (emphasis mine)

Procrastination and lollygagging are other words for this passivity. Still others may say, "I'm making plans to..." or "My intention is to..." How about when you think of a person and your intent is to visit, call or write them a letter and yet you never do. *Our unfulfilled intentions become our pretensions! As applied to one's living, people often convince themselves that their self-righteous pretensions,* although good intentions towards God and others, are sufficient and that any extracurricular activity outside of doing the church thing is not necessary. These people attend church service out of a sense of obligation to a societal influence, but neglect to consider that their religious obligation is to God alone. In this, they exhibit their social allegiance to a godless societal conscience!

Consider Your Ways

This statement applies to chapter one in which twice the word consider is mentioned and it appears three times in chapter two. In chapter one, Haggai exhorts the Hebrews to examine their heart, because the prophet knew that these people had placed a priority of their material things over the temple reconstruction, which was a bare stone altar at this time in history. For them, the altar became a token reminder of what was past and a glimmer of hope for a potential future. The Hebrews built mansions for themselves and ignored or put off the reconstruction of what was to become the second temple. In chapter 2:15, 18 Haggai again exhorted the Hebrews to consider the things of God and the temple. They were to sit down together and consult so as to establish a set work schedule, for they already knew what had to be done. They were also to reconstruct the neglected city of Jerusalem, which laid waste do to the result of war. Zerubabel, the Governor of the Hebrews, also possessed transcripts from King Darius, citing that all villages, which were initially seized by Babylon, where to be restored to the Hebrew nation. **Truth #243: Through a lifestyle of repentance, the saint does consider his carnal ways of self indulgence. In doing so, he makes a faith quality decision to live righteously, actively building upon the foundation of God's Word!**

Broken Spokes

The temple of God was then as it still remains today, the central hub of Israeli culture and society. Without this hub, the people of God were as broken spokes on a bicycle wheel, untethered, loose and flopping about. However, with this hub, they were as a properly trued wheel whose spokes were in place, taut and securely fastened. Form, structure, function and strength are byproducts of truth. Eventually, the Hebrews did set about to rebuild the temple. However, as they did so, they soon realized that they would not fit in with, nor were they suited for the wickedness of other nations. They had a place and as they worked, they were being shaped into the conformity of God's plan and will for their lives. **Truth #244: A lifestyle of repen-**

tance provides the saint the constructive activity which is conducive to righteousness. In this, he shall not dawdle aimlessly about or loiter at the cross! **Truth #245: A lifestyle of repentance reanimates the saint's heart [character] taking aim, focus and alignment at essential and pertinent matters of spiritual significance! Truth #246: Through a lifestyle of repentance, a saint builds his life upon the firm foundation of the prophets and of God's Word in three distinct ways:**

▶ 1. The Living Word: (True to Reason) Denotes and is therefore the autobiography of the character of God and the divine nature of Christ. A saint who, in faith, receives new life as found in the living Word, shall possess and demonstrate a new nature, because he has become a new creature. *(cf. 2 Pet. 1:4; Heb. 1:3; 2 Cor. 5:17; Jn. 5:24-26, 6:51, 63, 11:25-26)*

▶ 2. The Written Word: (True to Life) A saint becomes a law abiding citizen of heaven now, in his living, for God's Word abides in his heart. In this, he becomes an epistle known and read of all men, whose message is not written in ink, but by the Spirit of the living God. *(cf. Ps.119:11, 25-27, 32; 2 Cor. 3:2-3; Heb. 8:10)*

▶ 3. The Revealed (Rhema) Word: (True to Scripture) This is the inspired and quickened Spirit of the Word spoken to the saint's heart. Such exposition is the manifested power of the Word of God's righteousness to the saint.

Chapter 38
Repentance in the Book of Zechariah

From a Tradition to a Transition
In chapter 1:1-6, the Prophet Zechariah said, "God was sore displeased with your fathers." Verse 4 picks this point up again with this statement, "Be not as your fathers..." Verse 5 states, "Your fathers, where are they?" In each of our lives, there exists foundations or fashions of men upon which we have patterned our lives, which also include our established mind sets. Our thinking, our perceptions, our concepts and ideologies all are based upon the former days and former relationships, thereby making our present ways as demonstrations of previous progenitive ways! These are the result of societal influences and the example of our forefathers. Just because you might have done something the same way, in the same manner, in the same place, with the same people and at the same time, does not necessarily mean that it is of God or that it is the only method, manner, place, people or time! So many people live out their entire lives like assembly line robots. Few people want to lead; most choose to follow. Therefore, they continue to live out their lives, following their tradition and their past imitations and motivations.

We must break this yoke of parroting [Pauley want a cracker] mentality and shatter into crumbs, this cookie cutter manner of living! We must go from traditions to transitions! Transitions will require us to renew our mind and adopt a new lifestyle. Transitions will require us to change relationships, localities, thinking, and our manner of speech. Specifically, transitions will mandate that we exchange our carnality for godliness, because a transition is a right of passage!

As pertaining to fathers, a lifestyle of repentance renounces the old and stale, making room for the fresh and new. Strongholds of our past are demolished and in their place mighty spiritual fortresses are erected, for God is our refuge. **Truth #247: A life style of repentance is a right of passage from the old, stale traditions of our carnality to new transitions of godliness!**

Ishmael verses Isaac

Chapter 12:10-14 points to ancient family ties which date back to the days of Ishmael and Isaac. *(cf. Gen. 16 and 21)* Not surprisingly, the account of Abraham casting out Hagar, Sarai's Egyptian handmaid and her son Ishmael, along with the divorcement between the Israeli men and their Babylonian wives and their children, still fuels the Middle East conflict today! Like previously adjudicated trials, chapter 12 lists the compilation of righteous judgments which have been determined by the Judge of the universe against the hostilities of humanity who oppose Jerusalem.

An attorney would research previously adjudicated cases to establish a court precedent that may be beneficial to his current case. Well, Almighty God is about to repeat a precedent! It's known as Case Law. Specifically in verse 2, God says that Jerusalem shall once again become a cup of trembling to all nations round about present day Jerusalem, and to all those who have infiltrated God's holy city! All the nations shall mourn for the destruction which shall be very decisive and evident. Like a stone this is dropped in a pond, the ripple effect shall consume the entire earth. The day of the Lord shall be darkness and not light! Like the military coalition of the Gulf War, all the nations shall conspire against God and converge against Jerusalem! But this must be so, because what the Old city of Jerusalem is to the temporal, the New city of Jerusalem is to the eternal! *(cf. Rev. 21:2)*

Desert Storm

Revelations 9:20-21 and other verses in this investigation tell us of the fact that men shall refuse to repent, even in the face of God's wrath! However, here in Zechariah chapter 12, the citizens of Jerusalem were to do repentance on behalf of these adversarial nations, because of the carnage of their destruction. Just as Jerusalem crucified Jesus Christ, likewise, Jesus Christ shall destroy these other nations warring against Jerusalem upon His reappearance; and when He does so, then all the citizens of Jerusalem, past and present, shall mourn for their murder of the Son of God. *(cf. Zech. 12:9-10)*

I remember when in early January 1991, how my neighbors and I wept at the bombing sorties over Bagdad. A personal relationship with any Iraqi was not necessary to experience anguish and despair over the potential loss of the life of total strangers. We all are of the same mold! We are all flesh and blood, human beings, people and creations of Almighty God! *(cf. Zech. 12:1)* We all have the same needs, desires, joys and hurts. We have more things in common than we have not in common. The most common factor is that we are all spirit beings first with souls! Another thing in common that we all have is that we all are in need of salvation, to save us from our own devices of carnality. Once we pass away, then our true spirit selves and our soul, whether saved or not, shall continue to live throughout eternity, for we are all eternal, spirit beings. Therefore, a lifestyle of repentance assures us of eternal rest with Jesus Christ as citizens of God's kingdom for as He is, so shall every saint be as well. **Truth #248: A lifestyle of repentance is an exhibition of our love for our enemies, and their damned souls!** *(cf. Mat. 5:43-44)* Scripture tells us to pray for the peace of Jerusalem. *(Ps. 122:6)* Similarly, the saints of God are to pray for the temple of God, which they are! In other words, the saint of God must pray for himself, that he would be empowered by the sufficiency of God's grace, to live righteously before God. The saint who does so shall be sheltered from the wreckage caused by his carnality, for he is mindful of it and the outcome of his uprightness shall be divine protection in the day of God's wrath!

Chapter 39
Repentance in the Book of Malachi

Malachi, whose name means angel/messenger was the last of the Old Testament prophets and like all his predecessors, he was God's witness to a chosen people as well as to a corrupt priesthood. Prophets testified of God's providence and they witnessed His jurisdiction against the sinner and his sin. In like manner Malachi, like all the prophets before him, spoke of and preached the true intents of God's righteousness in His dealings with His chosen people and then the kind intentions of His grace concerning His church in the days of the Messiah, Jesus Christ, to whom all prophets bore witness.

The Burden of the Word is Repentance
Malachi 1:1
"The burden of the Lord to Israel by Malachi."

Since Malachi is sequentially, the last Old Testament prophet listed, I believe God's intent was to express one last time, the burden of His heart as sort of a final word of repentance in the last days of the Old Testament! In the book of Haggai, the people neglected the reconstruction of the temple for eighteen years after their release from Babylonian captivity. In Haggai, the temple eventually was rebuilt. Here in Malachi, the charge of the sanctuary and of the temple service was profaned and desecrated by the corrupt levitical priests. Repentance was most definitely in order! **Truth #249: Through a lifestyle of repentance, the saint keeps the charge of his sanctuary!**

Pangs of Death

In my capacity as a law enforcement officer, I've had several encounters with death. Many of which occurred in hospitals, where the dying person would make a final statement to another, moments before his passing. Often, the final plea was an obligation, which demanded a compliance by the survivor spoken to. As the book of Malachi closes out the last days of the Old Testament, it would be fair and safe too say that the burden of the Word has not changed!

Malachi 3:6
"For I am the Lord, I do not change; that is why you, O sons of Jacob , are not consumed."

Just as the survivor just mentioned, might honor and keep the death plea of the deceased, the people of God, as heirs of promise, have in time, become people of their broken promise, to obey God's commands! Specifically, by the priests who were obstinate towards Almighty God, and God's charge to them to keep their temple service. They were unreasonably determined to have their own way as rebellious children to their own father and as disobedient servants to their master! These men deserted their charge and duty to God. They were as thieves who ran from their master, but also ran away with their master's goods! **Truth #250: Through a lifestyle of repentance, the priestly saint heeds God's pangs of death to repent, because they are stiff warnings from God which must never be ignored!**

From A Reproof to a Reproach

These priests were derelict in their charge to keep the temple service! Like people today, they were also ignorant of righteousness, because they denied their carnality. Each of God's reproofs, as His expressed disapproval, was intended to invoke repentance and yet these priests took God's correction and instruction in righteousness as a reproach, something to be despised and detested. Like Esau, who found no place of repentance, these priests were totally ignorant of God's goodness which would have led them to repentance. Like the people of Chorazin and Bethsaida, who never repented, these priests would soon be brought to account for their impenitence. And so shall it be for every impenitent soul, who has ever lived and died in their sins! Now in the closing days of the New Testament, the burden of the Word of the Lord to impenitent humanity is still repentance! And as a death pang, humanity is obligated to comply.

Matthew 4:17
"And from that time, Jesus began to preach and to say, Repent, for the kingdom of heaven is at hand."

Luke 3:3 AMP
"And he (John the Baptist) went into all the country round about the Jordan, preaching the baptism of repentance (of hearty amending of their ways, with abhorrence of their past wrongdoing) unto the forgiveness of sin."

Luke 24:47 AMP
"And that repentance [with a view to and as a condition of] forgiveness of sins should be preached in His name to all nations, beginning from Jerusalem."

2 Peter 3:9 AMP
"The Lord does not delay and is not tardy or slow about what He promises, according to some people's conception of slowness, but He

is long-suffering (extraordinary patient) toward you, not desiring that any should perish, but that all should turn to repentance."

Romans 2:4 AMP
"Or are you [so blind as to] trifle and presume upon and despise and underestimate the wealth of His kindness and forbearance and long-suffering patience? Are you unmindful or actually ignorant [of the fact] that God's kindness is intended to lead you to repent (to change your mind and inner man to accept God's will)?"

Job 21:30 AMP
"That the evil man is [now] spared in the day of calamity and destruction, and they are led forth and away on the day of [God's] wrath?"

Psalm 37:37-38
"Mark the blameless man and behold the upright, for there is a happy end for the man of peace. As for transgressors, they shall be destroyed together; in the end, the wicked shall be cut off."

Zephaniah 2:1-3 AMP
"Collect your thoughts, yes, unbend yourselves [in submission and see if there is no shame and no consciousness of sin left in you]. O shameless nation [not desirous or desired]! [The time for repentance is speeding by like chaff whirled before the wind!] Therefore consider [your ways], before God's decree brings forth [the curse upon you], before the time [to repent] is gone like the drifting chaff, before the fierce anger of the Lord comes upon you-yes, before the day of the wrath of the Lord comes upon you! Seek the Lord [inquire for Him, inquire of Him, and require Him as the foremost necessity of your life], all you humble of the land who have acted in compliance with His revealed will and have kept His commandments;

seek righteousness, seek humility [inquire for them, require them as vital]. It may be you will be hidden in the day of the Lord's anger."

The Skill of Debate

There have been seasons in my life when I attempted to sell products door to door, and if you have ever had a pushy salesman force his sales pitch on you, whether in person or on the phone, you know what I mean. But I soon learned that I was not cut out to be a salesman! Although I would know the sales pitch and the product of question, I could not bring myself to close the deal. During sales training, I learned that there exists eight basic objections which I had to learn to overcome, if I were ever to be a successful salesman.

Well, there are nine objections that do appear in the book of Malachi in the form of defiance and repudiations, as declared by the contemptible priests! Their defiance was evident in their temple service which included a long list of repudiations, such as: their polluted [lame or sick] sacrifices, their obstinate heart, their infidelity and spouse abuse, their injustice, their utter rebellion, their theft and their overall nonsagacious conduct and behavior! In these, they disowned themselves from the love of God and denied themselves of His grace and mercy! So when you read these, do so with a hostile attitude and allow your imagination to bring to mind all the associated events in your life which might resemble those of the priests! In fact, whenever you read the Scripture, do so with animated intonations so as to put yourself in the midst of the event. Often, the meaning of Scripture is lost, when it is quickly read over or leafed through.

Objection #1:
In What Way Have You Loved Us?

Chapter 1:2 "I have loved you, says the Lord. Yet you say, How and in what way have You loved us?..."

These priests staggered at the commandments of God! In doing so, they questioned every rebuttal which Almighty God provided as an argument for His displeasure and against their carnality. Specifically, these impertinent priests dared to question God's abounding love for them. They failed to realize that God addressed their sin and not themselves. Had they responded in humility, such remorse would indicate their true repentance for in this, they would have known of their ignorance and acknowledged their carnality. However, these impudent priests were sold out to their carnal tendencies for they were in love with themselves and their selfish indulgences!

The sinner will question the existence of God and because he is a sinner, he would naturally question how a nonexistent God could love him. Perhaps you dear reader, have asked the identical question. Perhaps your self esteem is such, that you don't even love yourself. And if this is the case, then you can't accept God's love for yourself either. I can empathize with you, for I too have struggled with this hopelessness. But dear saint, please know that you must allow yourself to be exposed! You must allow the entrance of the truth of God's Word to reveal the wretched carnality within your soul. Presently, you think that you have peace, because you are left alone. But I want to let you know that this false peace is not the genuine true peace of righteousness! What you are embracing is a pseudo peace. Although it may hurt deep within, you must allow yourself to become transparent with the Holy Ghost through the light and life of God's Word. Perhaps your past was filled with violence, as mine was; and due to this assault against your soul, you have adopted an independent attitude and lifestyle. My friend, your hostilities in life are but the seed tops of a full crop of embedded carnality which must be mowed and suppressed!

Objection #2:
How and in What Way Have We Despised Your Name?

Chapter 1:6, 12 *"...O priests who despise My Name. You say, How and in what manner have we despised your Name?"*

If you want to discredit somebody, attack their character for in doing so, you discredit their name. Since a man's name is equated to the strength of his character, defamation and scandal go along way towards the usurpation of the man slighted. The fact that these priests attacked God's Name, denotes a conspiracy to overthrow the established theocratic authority or rule. So the point is, whenever someone despises God's Name, in effect, he is usurping God's authority and rule in his life! Not only did these priests despise God's Name, but in their scorn they also blasphemed it. Because these priests had no regard for God's commandments, they possessed no appreciation for His Name! Scripture tells us that Almighty God magnifies His Word, even above His Name. He expects His saints to also magnify His Word above theirs. When the saints do so, God's Word becomes theirs and the result will be that they esteem His Name above every name under heaven, for there is no other name under heaven given by which men ought to be saved. *(cf. Ps. 138:2; Acts 4:12)*

Objection #3:
Since There is no Profit in It, Why Bother?

Chapter 3:14 *"You have said, It is useless to serve God; and what profit is it if we keep His ordinances and walk gloomily...?"*

Many people whom God has called to the ministry, have opted for the glit and glimmer of secular life, and all for the money! Their selfish desires fuel their pursuit for the material thing, and often at the expense of others. Such was the case with these corrupt priests, who oppressed the people for their own gainful motives. These fail to realize that Almighty God would hold them to account for the squandered gifts which He has placed in them.

Objection #4: A Polluted Altar

Chapter 1:7, 12 *"...How have we polluted it [altar] and profaned You?"*(brackets mine)

These filthy priests wallowed in spiritual vomit! Since they offered polluted sacrifices which were taken by force or coercion, Almighty God considered them as a table smeared with the vomit of carnality. The putrid stench that rose from the altar only reflected the putrefaction within the table of their hearts! *(cf. Is. 28:8)* The sight of this regurgitation, evinced the gut wrenching discontent for the things of God!

Objection #5:
What a Drudgery and Weariness This Is!

Chapter 1:12-13 *"You say also, Behold, what a drudgery and weariness this is...you have brought that which was taken by violence, or the lame or the sick; this you bring as an offering!..."*

These dawdling priests allowed themselves to become fat and lazy on the soiled offerings of others, which were fruits of their violence. There is an adage which says, "Absolute power corrupts and power corrupts absolutely." These priests were corrupted absolutely, because their self indulgence was evident in their position and their ill-gotten possessions. It reminds me of the tendency of some who are in positions of authority to become fat headed with pride. I can recall other Marine Drill Instructors and other law enforcement officers who had such an attitude. We called it, the "Big Hat" syndrom or the "Big Badge" syndrom. In both occasions, these men were an offense to myself and others in uniform who were not out to make a "big show" of themselves and abuse their position and the public. Even in ministry, I've been told by some that they tend to become fat headed with pride, because of the demands others place on them for their skillful, scriptural oratory. Scripture tells us that pride goes before destruction, and a haughty spirit before a fall. *(Prov. 16:18)* Watch out, thou man of God!

Objection #6:
Why Does He Reject Our Offerings?
Chapter 2:14 "Yet you ask, Why does He reject our offerings?..."

Cain slew his brother Abel not because Abel was good, but because his offering was acceptable to God and Cain's offering was rejected. So in a heat of rage, Cain killed Abel over religion. And so it remains today, that denominations as well as warring nations kill each other due to a religious spirit! Spiritually speaking, these priests did in fact wear Cain's shoes! Although they never offered anybody as a human sacrifice, they did however, kill the relationship between God and themselves. God rejected their offerings because of their carnal disposition, which reflected the sentiments of their calloused heart.

Objection #7:
In What Way Have We Wearied Him?
Chapter 2:17 "You have wearied the Lord with your words. Yet you say, In what way have we wearied Him?"

Have you ever been worn out by the incessant prodding of empty words spoken to you or about you by another? I certainly have. How about the individual who possesses no integrity, because he lacks credibility? These priests fit this description to a tee. Their opportunity to serve God at His altar was ignored and in so doing, they forfeited the occasions to maintain their credibility. As we learned earlier, a man's credibility is the foundation of his integrity! Therefore, every chance to enhance credibility only strengthens integrity! These priests failed in both. The fact that these priests said that their temple service was a drudgery and weariness *(1:13)*, intimates that perhaps they themselves were weary of doing that which was good and right. Who knows, perhaps during the course of their lives, outside of their temple service, carnality obtained a stronghold due to some persistent situation which might have tarnished their collective priesthood. I mean, it happens with me! Somewhere and at some time, certain things occur that seem to challenge my faith in God so much so that it seems like I am chained to a seaward cliff side and pounded by the ocean swells crashing against the cliff! The season of these assaults against my heart seems never ending, in that time seems to drag by. However, because God has given me a will, as the executive faculty of my soul, I can choose to lean more upon God's grace or I may choose to stray from His grace. Either way, it's all about authority. I am either in authority of, or I allow myself to be under the authority of. The decision is strictly mine, as it is yours. *(cf. Gal. 6:9)*

Objection #8: How Shall We Return?

Chapter 3:7-9 "...But you say, How shall we return? Will a man rob God? Yet you have robbed Me. But you say, In what way have we robbed You? You have withheld your tithes and offerings. You are cursed with the curse, for you are robbing Me, even this whole nation?"

Without a road map, a driver could easily get lost. To remedy this, he might ask a police officer, How do I return? Apparently, these priests had lost their way. Like Esau, who forfeited his birthright for a pot of stew, these priests lost their legacy. Consequently, they too found no place of repentance as Esau! All they had to do was ask God for guidance; but they would not. It is for this reason that Almighty God commands all men to repent. Humanity must learn righteousness, for God's Word is the word of His righteousness! If repentance is not taught as a judgment against the carnality of one's soul, as commanded, then there is no suppressant of one's carnality! *(cf. Heb. 5:13)*

Objection #9:
In What Way Have We Robbed You?

These priests robbed God! Can you imagine that? How can a mortal man rob God who owns the cattle on a thousand hills and the hills themselves? Traditional interpretation declares that we rob God through the withholding of our tithes and offerings. *(Mal. 3:10)* But as we have learned earlier, that the reference to "meat in my house" applies to the salt of righteousness within your house, for you are the house of God and the temple of the Holy Ghost. It is evident then that these priests had lost their savor, that quality of righteousness and uprightness within their souls and their hearts. Therefore, as far as God was concerned, he imposed this indictment against them for the crimes of their carnality which Almighty God had argued.

Not only did they rob God, but so did the entire nation of Israel, both the northern and southern kingdoms! If God were talking about money alone, then it is evident that the priests would have been billionaires, for they would have pauperized the people. However, if God spoke of their corrupt temple service, as an external demonstration of the internal carnal issues of their hearts, then the entire nation would have been deprived of proper spiritual leadership also. Therefore, of a truth, should the saint get his heart right first, then all the virtues of godliness shall emanate from his godly heart. This includes tithes and offerings, as well as his upright character in God. After all, before anyone can change outwardly, they first must be renewed inwardly, for God loves a cheerful giver, whose heart is in his giving! *Almighty God is not a repository for laundered money! He is however, the banker for undefiled faith!*

I recall when I was a young Marine living in the barracks on base. Occasionally, someone would invade another's privacy and violate another's property by theft. This theft occurred repeatedly by one individual who obviously had a problem. But before the thief was apprehended, the morale of the men in the entire barracks began to wain, so much so, that we ended up accusing each other! The point is that these priests *shanghaied* the spiritual integrity of the entire nation, all because of their selfish indulgences as demonstrated before God and the people. The result was a dread among the people!

Answer a Question With a Question

Chapter 3:13 "...Yet you say, What have we spoken against You?"

As the topic for this segue indicates, there is an art or skill of debate. And it is common knowledge that if you desire to turn a dispute around to your favor, just respond to a question asked you with an answer that is also a question! In a courtroom, for instance, an attorney would present a question to the witness pertaining to the case in question by prefacing the question with, "I'm sure you would agree..." or "Wouldn't you agree that..." Furthermore, he would also insert, as a backside phrase to an initial question, "...now wouldn't you agree" or "...couldn't it be?" This technique refutes the source of the specifics of the initial inquiry and at the same time casts a shadow of doubt in the mind of the witness, so as to strengthen the view of generality postulated by the other side. These priests, who were the forerunner of the Pharisees and who were trained in the law, had attempted to refute every question presented to them by Malachi, God's Prophet! It's as if they retained each others legal counsel to discredit God's argument against them, just as two opposing attorneys would provide in court! Their conduct then gives credence to Abraham who staggered not at the promise [command] of God, for he never filed an appeal against God as these priests have done. Therefore, it is important that the saints of God be careful not to question or debate with God's instructions in righteousness for their lives.

The carnal mind is an unrenewed mind and shall remain so as long as people do not place a value on the Word of God! People would rather justify their carnality by denying it! What arrogance to think that anyone can sue God as at law or to call into question His precious Word! People must place a value on the Word of God otherwise, they will not value and claim it as their own nor the minister who presents it!

Notes:

Chapter 40

The Seven Furnaces of Mystery Babylon

Throughout the years, Egypt has been likened to the land of sin for the New Testament Church, and that those who backslide have returned to Egypt themselves. For those who still reside in Egypt, the bondage of their sin insinuates that their skimpy vegetation diet in sin, consists of cucumbers and onions. Whereas others, who have been delivered from Egypt, have opted for the meat and vegetables of Babylonian captivity. For these, the creature comforts of a good feed that quells the hunger pangs of a self indulgent lifestyle are all that is necessary according to their view of godliness, whose god is their belly! *(cf. Phil. 3:18-19)* Where the former denotes hard bondage of a hard life in sin, the latter connotes an indoctrinated concept of Babylonian feasting, which dulls the senses and erects mental passivity and carnal tendencies. Since the mind is neither active or passive, people determine for themselves their own state of mind. Consequently, whatever the mind is fed, the resulting knowledge shall be the outcome of its ingestion or indigestion, which ever the case may be. What you are about to experience in the following pages, is a revelation of God which He has taught me regarding the seven furnaces of Mystery Babylon. In years past, when I was just a young buck in the Lord, I was informed by a well meaning Baptist brother that the Authorized King James Version is the only translation of Scripture that Almighty God has approved of for man's use, and that all other translations were forbidden, due to their diluted translations of the authorized text. Although I've always had my preferred versions for study, I had no working knowledge of Scripture at that time to refute him with, so I allowed him his opinion. However, I had a check in my heart that this guy was about a half bubble off plumb! Specifically, the Scripture he presented was *Psalm 12:6* which states,

"For the words of the Lord are pure words, as silver tried in a furnace of earth, purified seven times." Other verses he presented to me were as follows:

I recall that this conversation, occurred in the spring of 1979 and through the years since, I have often wondered about what he had said to me regarding *Psalm 12:6*. So two years ago, while reading through the Psalms, I progressed to *Psalm 12*. This time, I wanted answers! I asked God to teach me the significance of this particular verse, as I was tired of being stumped by it for lack of specific knowledge. So I asked the Lord, my God to answer some basic questions which are as follows:

• 1. Does this verse mean too say that there exists seven furnaces on or of the earth?

• 2. Does this verse mean too say that one furnace was used seven times?

• 3. Or does this verse tell us that there are seven differing furnaces and if so, what does each furnace represent or convey to humanity?

It is common knowledge that "Mystery Babylon" as found in Scripture, is described as a harlot riding on a scarlet beast and in some camps of prophetic thought, *Revelation 17 verse 5*, which portrays Mystery Babylon, is believed to be the Roman Catholic Church. But the fact that Mystery Babylon is found in the book of Revelation, which is future tense, as far as its preceding Scriptural books go, tells me that it still exists today and has survived throughout the millennia in some insidious fashion or another.

Case Law:
To Establish a Precedent as a Basis for an Argument

To properly develop any argument, which is intended to convince others of truth, requires that such truth be established upon life, reason and Scripture. Once this is done, then the preponderance of evidentiary truth from each of these categories should achieve its intended purpose, because the human mind requires such convincing truth. Otherwise, the mind feels cheated. So I have endeavored to layout my case of these seven iron furnaces for argument, apologetically speaking. I hope that you would agree and be convinced and amazed as I.

Scripture teaches that there are seven *seals,* seven *trumpets,* seven *vials,* seven *Spirits* of God and seven *plagues* spoken of in the book of Revelation. The seven seals seem to address a long period of time, perhaps hundreds or thousands of years in history. The seven trumpets possibly denotes an intermediate passage of time, say about one hundred years, while the seven vials seem to correspond with the seven plagues which are the shortest time frame of all, the last three and one half years of the tribulation period. And the seven Spirits of God, which possibly represent the multiplicity of God's concern in the affairs of men. Each possess a common denominator namely, that of human participation and God's intervention.

The providence of Almighty God can be seen in the events and the experiences of humanity. This observation therefore, provides evidence of His existence and intervention in and throughout man's history. Pertaining to *Psalm 12:6,* Scripture seems to indicate that there may be seven furnaces as well, and that their common denominator is also human involvement. Therefore, I make this postulation that there are in fact, seven iron furnaces and each furnace represents a process of time and a right of passage in the span of an individual's life! *The fact that Scripture describes a furnace to be made of iron is significant, because man's iron will, is his dogged determination to live carnally. Therefore man's carnality necessitates an iron furnace to counter the damaging effects of this destructive fire within his soul! In this sense and of a truth, as iron sharpens iron, so does a man sharpen the countenance of his friend.* After all, didn't Jesus Christ call us friends? This is in keeping with repentance as the doctrine of God. So let's embark on a guided tour of these seven furnaces of Mystery Babylon with the Holy Ghost as our tour guide.

The mere mention of seven furnaces is not some attempt at a poetic flair. Rather, God has shown me their existence as found in Scripture. They actually do exist, spiritually! Since man is first a spirit being, who has a soul and who lives in a physical body, these furnaces then apply to the soul of man, and at specified seasons during his life!

Each furnace, as you shall see, directly correlates to a specific Babylonian influence that is indigenous within the soul of carnal man; and no matter how or in what season these furnaces appear, each exists to address the warfare between good and evil caused by carnality. Carnality as an intrusive demonic entity, has its roots which date back to the garden of Eden, and one of its first tentacles is seen in the Tower of Babel! You see, since man is first a spirit and has a soul and although his body may be fragile and therefore temporal, the spirit and soul within continues to live, for we were all created as eternal beings. As they say, "You may kill the body, but you can't kill the spirit." This even applies to the demonic. Therefore, through the use of these furnaces, Almighty God purifies His Word in the lives of His saints from Babylonian practices, thereby saving them from His wrath, because Jesus Christ is coming back for a glorious church without spot or wrinkle or *any such thing! Just as each of the temple vessels and other utensils were covered with their own sackcloth bag, likewise, any such thing that should be covered with the blood of Christ within a soul, also speaks of the entrenchments of carnal tendencies within that soul!* **Hallelujah!!**

The objective of this Holy Ghost inspired tour is to discover these furnaces, but also to learn of their explanations for the following reasons.

- 1. To reveal each of the furnaces and to explain their application in a saint's walk.
- 2. To help each saint to determine for himself, just which furnace he may find himself to be in presently and to reveal the furnaces he has already gone through or has yet to experience.
- 3. To enable the saint to discern a specific furnace in the life of another.
- 4. To appreciate the work of righteousness as God purifies His Word within the saint.
- 5. To expose the ancient Babylonian practices that still reside, as carnality, within the hearts and minds of humanity.
- 6. To reveal through Scripture, the insidious, demonic attachments of Babylonian influences, by tracking down their existence in the lives of those mentioned in Scripture.
- 7. To assist the saint in the process of his sanctification from this worldly Babylonian system, so that he may be glorified in the next.

▶ **Furnace #1: Fear to be Replaced by Faith (Trust)**

Careful! Don't Get Incinerated!

As already stated, the mysterious, demonic entities originated after the fall of Adam and Eve. *(Gen. 3:6)* Consequently, Almighty God arraigned or indicted the man, Adam, for his sin and expelled him from the garden of Eden. *(Gen. 3:23-24, 6:1-2)* Through the passage of time, literally hundreds of years, a man named Nimrod ascended to power and he was instrumental in the construction of the Tower of Babel. *(Gen. 10:8-10, 11:1-9)* It was during his reign, that the Babylonian civilization grew to become the ancient Assyrian Empire which is present day Iraq. Since its birth, Mystery Babylon has existed spiritually in one form or another throughout the history of mankind.

Abram, the son of Terah, was born in Ur of the land of the Chaldeans. *(Gen. 12:28)* He and his family lived under the strong influence of Babylon. They eventually relocated to a place known as Haran, which means in Hebrew, "a place of burning with anger." *(Gen. 12:31-32)* Haran also means, "to glow, melt, burn, dry up, be angry, kindle." Again, Haran was a specific Babylonian city. *(Gen. 12:4)* Abram had a hot headed brother, whose name was also Haran. *(Gen. 11:26-28)* Apparently, Haran was so named for his volatile disposition, which possibly reflected the oppressive living conditions of Abram's family in Babylon.

It has been said, "That you can take the boy out of country, but you can't take the country out of the boy." Well, this seems to apply to Abram here in Babylon. All he and his family ever knew were the Babylonian influences. Scripture seems to indicate that Abram and his family did not participate with the Babylonian idol worship to Molech, a fire god; because Terah, Abram's father, took his family to Haran, just as you or I would relocate to other venues to start over, and in Abram's case to possibly escape a hostile environment.

Since Molech, the premier Babylonian fire god, was worshiped throughout the land of Babylon, it stands to reason that a myriad of furnaces would have been constructed for this very purpose. These furnaces must have been imposing to look at, as they loomed high above the landscape. Graveyards were numerous and in close proximity to them. It was here, in these bone yards, that mass graves were dug to bury the charred, skeletal remains of children who were offered to Molech. The stench of burning flesh permeated the atmosphere! And the cries of innocent children, who were as fodder for the god, Molech, rang in the ears of moms and dads everywhere! So considering this, it is reasonable to assume that Abram and his family were very familiar with furnaces and their deadly purpose. Possibly, the Chaldeans threatened Terah, Abram's father, with their intent to incinerate Abram's family, unless they worshiped Molech as all the rest of society did. Incidently, according to the date line of Scripture, history shows the existence of this Babylonian influence in 624 B.C. and again in 580 B.C. An excellent example of this is found in *2 Kings 23* and *Daniel 3*.

Eventually, God commanded Abram, now grown, to leave his family and to travel to Si'chem in the plain of Moreh, where God would appear to Abram upon his arriving. *(cf. Gen. 12:1-7)* In *Genesis 15:12-17*, God caused a deep sleep to fall upon Abram sometime after Abram had placed meat on a make shift altar. While he slept, a smoking furnace and a burning lamp appeared, which moved about and between the sacrificial pieces, as in a figure eight. Abram was very familiar with these two Babylonian instruments of death, as they forged a terror of death by fire into Abram's psyche and that of his family. God used these two symbols of fear, because He knew that Abram would respond to them! God wanted to teach Abram that the fear of the Lord, must replace the fear of carnal man and his evil devices.

A more current illustration for us today would be the holocaust of World War II. Any surviving Jew today, would still be tormented in the theater of his/her mind by all the haunts and flashbacks of this inhumane atrocity! Another illustration would be the flinch of any victimized person, who has been repeatedly violated emotionally, mentally or physically at the heavy hand of an influential other in their life. Or an animal, which has been beaten or tortured by a cruel owner or an abusive institutional system. **Truth #251: Through a lifestyle of repentance, the bondage of fear and torment caused by past experiences, are replaced with a healthy understanding of the fear of the Lord!** This then identifies and describes the first iron furnace to be

Faith, because we trust God to enable us to overcome the carnal ghosts of our past.

Trust, which is synonymous with faith, means to give another the right to speak into your life and this trust must be earned! Just because the majority rules, does not make it right and the minority necessarily wrong. Peer pressure is often an abusive experience in life. A saint must never allow this pressure to remain, rule or dominate as a stronghold or vain imagination. If he does, then the haunt of the imagined thing of his past, shall continue to usurp the attempts of the Holy Ghost to emancipate the saint from this carnality! God provides freedom, that way of escape, which enables each saint to stand up to and against the frequent replay of past hostile encounters. Truly, what the devil intended for our harm or demise, God has meant for our good! *(cf. Gen. 50:20)* Therefore, as saints of God, we must come to a place and time where we will give God our evil haunts and when we do, then our loving, merciful Father shall bring to pass or cause to occur, a salvation experience from this particular bondage of fear. No longer shall this fear be locked in any compartment of your carnality!

2 Timothy 1:7 AMP
"For God did not give us a spirit of timidity (of cowardice, of craven and cringing and fawning fear), but [He has given us a spirit] of power and of love and of calm and well-balanced mind and discipline and self control."

Isaiah 41:10 AMP
"Fear not [there is nothing to fear], for I am with you,; do not look around in terror and be dismayed, for I am your God. I will strengthen and harden you to difficulties, yes, I will help you; yes, I will hold you up and retain you with My [victorious] right hand of rightness and justice."

1 Corinthians 10:13 AMP

"For no temptation (no trial regarded as enticing to sin), [no matter how it comes or where it leads] has overtaken you and laid hold on you that is not common to man [that is, no temptation or trial has come to you that is beyond human resistance and that is not adjusted and adapted and belonging to human experience, and such as man can bear]. But God is faithful [to His Word and to His compassionate nature], and He [can be trusted] not to let you be tempted and tried and assayed beyond your ability and strength of resistance and power to endure, but with the temptation He will [always] provide the way out (the means of escape to a landing place), that you may be capable and strong and powerful to bear up under it patiently."

▶ Furnace #2: The Furnace of Repentance and Sanctification

This iron furnace includes restraints and warnings against carnality in the forms of religiosity, vain curiosity and presumptuous sins of the flesh. The foundational text is Exodus chapter 19:1-25. What an iron furnace was to melting hardened metals, this spiritual furnace is to reconciliation of the iron will of carnal men! *(cf. 1 Kgs. 8:51; 2 Cor. 5:19-20)*

Getting Bloody in the Spirit

Exodus 19, finds the Hebrew people at the base of Mount Sinai approximately fifty [Pentecost] days into their journey from Egyptian bondage. It was here that Moses made his ascent up the mountain of God to minister unto the Lord, his God. The Almighty told Moses to instruct the people to prepare for a divine visitation in three days time, for the Lord, Himself would descend. Moses was to instruct the people to make their personal and corporate preparations in advance of their day of visitation. Specifically, that they were to wash their clothing. *(vs.10)*

The Ten Commandments were given fifty days after the first

Passover. This fifty day passage of time was a precedent for the future New Testament day of Pentecost as found in the book of Acts. *(cf. Ex. 12:11, 13, 13:1-14)* The people accepted the Ten Commandments as the divine charter for their nation, and they obeyed Moses' instructions of preparation. Herein is revealed a type and shadow. Particularly, that the smoke of God's Shekinah Glory as it descended upon the people from atop Mount Sinai, favors the dove that descended upon Jesus Christ; just as the cloven tongues of fire which descended upon the one hundred twenty in the upper room, as well as the saints who will return with Jesus Christ! *(cf. Rev. 19:14)* Mind you, this smoke of God's presence must not to be confused with the cigarette smoke of church attending, nicotine addicts or the polluted flame of carnal men!

Blazing Your Own Trail

The word, *Sinai* means, "to inscribe, to score with a mark as a tally or record, to enumerate, recount, to celebrate, commune, count, declare, number, pen knife, reckon, scribe, shew forth, speak, tell, talk, writer." Mount Sinai was so named for the multitude of thorny bushes that over spread it round about. (Matthew Henry's commentary, page 122, column 1) Moses had to blaze his own trail through these briars as he climbed. This no doubt caused some blood letting from Moses, as he ascended the mount! Interestingly, a ram was found by Abram on Mount Sinai with its horns caught in a thorn bush, which portrayed the crown of thorns that encircled the head of Christ on Mount Calvary! **Truth #252: The Holy Ghost is saying that the renewal of one's mind along with the regeneration and the reconciliation of the soul is a trail to blaze through the unchartered thickets of carnality by the individual, alone!**

Therefore, the second iron furnace is identified and described as a Lifestyle of Repentance and Sanctification.

God has contempt for the pavilions, the palaces and the

monuments to man's arrogance! So He selected a mountain of His righteousness to rise above the mountains of man's carnality, for this mountain was to be the pulpit, from which He would speak. Mountains exalt the very creative power of an Almighty Creator, just as any multistory, corporate building would exalt the affluence of carnal man and the prosperity of civilizations. The glory of salvation's deliverance, is to experience the very presence of God! We must never presume that we know more than God, for He knows that we are but dust. And all things invented by man or created, constructed or designed by him are temporal as he is worldly.

But getting back to the Hebrew preparations, it is implied that their repentance of sins was emphasized by the activity of washing their clothes *(19:10)*. Just as a proper attire would be worn in the audience of a great man in the natural, likewise, a clean heart must be worn before a great God! In these closing days of the end times of the age of the gentiles, there looms another one world government on the horizon. It's Mystery Babylon, as a New World Order. This new world order shall engulf the entire globe in and through which all inhabitants of the earth must ascribe to. It is very obvious that the success of this Babylonian system to remove the Ten Commandments from our existing government institutions, from our schools, and even from the hearts of men, shall in its place, proclaim their decree that once again, all must bend the knee and worship Molech, and those that refuse to shall be incinerated! Only this time, there won't be an actual furnace, although things could change, seeing as how the furnaces used in the death camps of World War II still exist! But the furnace of standing your ground in saving faith that legally binds you to God through a relationship with Jesus Christ, shall be applied by those who are opposed to God and His Christ! It is for this reason that we must submit our soul's to God's perfect will and allow ourselves to be put in the furnace of repentance, ahead of time. Otherwise, we will cave to the external pressures applied by the opposition of faith, because such enticements will lure the flesh. **Truth #253: Through a lifestyle of repentance, the saint can stand his ground on the basis of his saving faith in Christ and his compliance to the terms and conditions of the Word of God. In doing so, he will be able to stand against the heated violence that shall be applied to him by those who are opposed to God and His Christ!**

▶ **Furnace #3: Furnace of Forensic Cross-Examination**
Proverbs 17:3
"The refining pot is for silver, and the furnace for gold: but the Lord trieth the hearts."

Proverbs 27:21
"As the refining pot is for silver, and the furnace for gold; so is a man to his praise."

Malachi 3:3
"And he shall sit as a refiner and a purifier of silver: and he shall purify the sons of Levi, and purge them as gold and silver, that they may offer unto the Lord an offering in righteousness."

James 1:23-24
"For if any be a hearer of the word, and not a doer, he is like unto a man beholding his own face in a glass: For he beholdeth himself and goeth his way, and straightway forgetteth what manner of man he was."

The Trial of One's Heart

The purpose of this iron furnace is for a man to determine for himself what he will do with his life and with the gifts and callings given him. As *Romans 12:1* states we are to be "...living sacrifices, holy and acceptable unto God which is our reasonable service." This however, is a life long process of sanctification. Only through faith and repentance will people be able to present themselves in righteousness, for righteousness is an out flow of saving faith and repentance. They go hand in hand. *(cf. Acts 20:21)* Without faith, why should one repent, but with faith, repentance is essential, because faith tells us that there is a living God, while repentance tells us that we are sinners who need God!

Truth #254: Whereas, Jesus Christ is described as the saint's advocate, this furnace involves a cross examination process which purifies what we think we know by purging all bias and short sightedness, to reveal what we really don't know. What is left is the truth that we should know, and it is this truth that shall set us free! Therefore, the Word of God is to the saint, as a defense attorney who cross examines him in court. In this, the word of His righteousness is the means of a cross examination process to purify or qualify what faith he thinks he has, to reveal the faith that he doesn't have and to teach him the faith that he should have and to expose the misunderstood faith that he presently has! This therefore identifies and describes the third furnace to be a Forensic Cross Examination of all that is generally known and to acquire that which should known and not just believed.

▶ Furnace #4: Increase Your Property Value
Zechariah 2:5
"For I, saith the Lord, will be unto her a wall of fire round about, and will be the glory in the midst of her."

Isaiah 31:9
"...whose fire is in Zion, and His furnace in Jerusalem."

Matthew 11:12
"And from the days of John the Baptist until now, the kingdom of heaven suffereth violence and the violent take it by force."

Luke 11:22-26
"When a strong man armed keepeth his palace, his goods are in peace: but when a stronger man than he shall come upon him, and overcome him, he taketh from him all his armor wherein he trusteth, and divideth his spoils..." (cf. Ps. 21:9, 68:29; Rev. 11:5)

The city of Jerusalem in Israel today is God's iron furnace! Unknowingly, all the violence that is occurring there now, is stoking the fire of man's future destruction! It was prepared for the day of God's wrath. God is a jealous God and a consuming fire! He will make His enemies as fuel for the fire of His indignation, for whoever assails Jerusalem does so to their own peril! Jerusalem is the old city of King David. However, it shall become the furnace of God to consume the carnality of impenitent man. Once the purpose of this old city is complete, then the New city of Jerusalem, the city of the Great King and God shall descend. Of a truth, God is keeping house, even today!

There is also an altar in Jerusalem. It's called Calvary. But prior to calvary, there was another altar. It was found in Solomon's Temple. *(cf. 2 Chron. 5:1)* Here upon this altar, blood sacrifices were continually being offered in praise and honor to God. At Calvary, Jesus Christ, the sacrificial Lamb of God, also offered Himself up as an atonement for the sins of humanity. His death on calvary increased the property value of Jerusalem, the furnace of God. Through His death, Jesus set the example for all to follow. His instruction was then as it is now, to deny self, to mortify the flesh and all its propensities, and to take up our cross daily and follow after him. *(cf. Lk. 9:22-27; Rom. 8:13)*
Truth #255: When self is denied through a lifestyle of repen-

tance, and the cross of Christ is taken up, the devil and the host of Babylonian entities are overcome. In this, the saint's own personal property value is greatly increased as well! Otherwise, this earthen vessel called a physical body and all its passions remain the domain of filth and vermin. What is left is just a poorly maintained house in a run down community of carnal humanity. What a pity! This then identifies and describes the fourth furnace, known as Increased Property Value.

▶ Furnace #5: The Righteous Judgment of the Church
Ezekiel 22:17 AMP
"And the word of the Lord came to me saying, Son of man, the house of Israel has become to Me scum and waste matter. All of them are bronze and tin and iron and lead in the midst of the furnace; they are the dross of silver. Therefore thus says the Lord God: Because you have all become scum and waste matter, behold therefore, I will gather you [O Israel] into the midst of Jerusalem."

Hebrews 10:30b
"...And again, the Lord shall judge His people."

Overcoming One's Hardness of Carnality

According to classical Greek Mythology, the first era of the world, was a *Golden Age* when Saturn reigned and truth, innocense, and ideal happiness prevailed. There was no law, nor was their a need for any; there were no weapons, no wars. The Romans commemorated this era every year in their festival of the Saturnalia. This *Golden Age* was followed by the *Silver Age* and then the *Bronze (Brass) Age*. In every age, men and their fallen conditions were a little bit worse than before. The classical Greeks and Romans called their own period the Iron Age and thought that things were getting worse all the time. (The Volume Library, page 1325, column 2)

Daniel 2:32-33 AMP
"As for this image, its head was of fine gold, its breasts and its arms of silver, its belly and its thighs of bronze, its legs of iron its feet partly of iron partly of clay [the baked clay of the potter]."

The research text and the scriptural texts above, lists several metals in a descending order of value. Since spiritual truths parallel physical realities, let's now look at what the scriptural equivalent would be to this mythology. On a descending scale of value and use, the chosen people of God depreciated in value and worth, at least as far as their usefulness to God. However, in their devalued state or condition, they remained of some value and of some use in this unrighteous world and to the wicked who populate it. So let's examine the following metals as metallurgists, using some principles of forensic investigation. Aside of the more apparent qualities and identification of these metals, I selected the spiritual meanings of each, as they reflect the condition or state of a carnal heart, which tend to bleed into a person's character, for after all, people are known by such.

DROSS: means, "to retreat, to apostatize, backslider, refuse, slag residue of melted metal, scum and waste matter." Dross is good for nothing in its impurities. However, when purified, it is useful once again. (Strong's Exhaustive Concordance Heb. ref. #5472, page 82)

BRASS: (bronze) means, "bold impudence, effrontery." It is of less value but is still of good use. Scriptures relate that brass represents man. *(cf. Ezek. 40:3, 22:18; Dan. 239)*

BRAZEN: means, "showing no shame, bold, impudent, harsh and piercing sound."

BRAZEN FACED: means, "a brazen expression, shameless."

TIN: means, "to denote cheapness, baseness, spuriousness: illegitimate, bastard, not true or genuine, false, counterfeit, artificial." It is still of some use. It also infers to divide asunder. (Strong's Exhaustive Concordance Heb. ref #914, page 19)

IRON: means, "as cutting, firm, unyielding (iron will), stubbornness, cruel, merciless, firm strength, power, rusts very rapidly in moist air, salty air or water, but still of good use. (Strong's Exhaustive Concordance Heb. ref. #1270, page 24) Iron represents war and contention. *(cf. Job 20:24; Prov. 27:17; Eccl 9:18; Dan. 2:40)*

LEAD: means, "soft and pliable to evil but resistant to good, hard to move or lift, sluggish, dull, depressed, dispirited, gloomy." LEAD is to the dogged pursuit of carnality as gold is to undefiled faith. (Strong's Exhaustive Concordance Heb. ref. #6080, page 90)

Gold of Faith and the Silver of Carnality
Ezekiel 22:18, 20
"...they even the dross of silver,...as they gather silver..."

Silver is of less value than gold, but is still very useful. It is also a lesser metal than gold. It becomes tarnished, when exposed to light as used in photography, for example.

There is a Golden Age and a Silver Age! As applied to Ezekiel, the house of Israel had slipped into a Silver Age and continued to decline through idolatry. *(cf. Ezek. 22:1-31; Dan. 3:1)* Consequently, the city of Jerusalem became a reproach to all the gentile nations and were mocked accordingly. *(cf. Ezek. 22:4)* They even were as brass, because God was not caught off guard by the brazen faced ways of His chosen people. God has a plan of redemption for mankind, however, man's carnality, this plan requires the use of an iron furnace. Again, just as the use of an iron furnace is intended for the iron will of man's carnality, likewise the silver of redemption corresponds to the declining ages of man's selfish indulgences! It is for this reason that silver compares to redemption, and why brazen man is redeemed from the brass of his carnality.

A Silver Age is any period of progress and of prosperity, which is a lessor degree than that of the previous Golden Age. It is the second age of an unrighteous world, which is inferior to the first, which is righteous. Therefore, the Golden Age is to faith as the Silver Age is to carnality! The Golden Age existed before the fall of man, and it shall exist once again, in the lives of those who are of an audacious faith now! The Golden Age shall also exist during the millennial reign of Christ here on earth and for all eternity, once God's plan of salvation for the ages is complete.

The Silver Age as well as the other "metallic" ages pertains to carnality as an atrophy in the way of life. When we reject God's plan of redemption, we are to him as scum and waste matter which is fit for the scrap heap. Through our fault, the house which we occupy is permitted to deteriorate, due to a lack of spiritual strength and renovation which the Word of God provides. Having repentance towards God and possessing faith in Jesus Christ, prevents this atrophy from taking place. The process of renewing our minds beyond a conversion experience is essential for spiritual growth, strength and prosperity, all of which speaks of a regenerated soul. *(cf. Rev. 14:12)* **Truth #256: Through a lifestyle of repentance, the saint demonstrates, by and through his faith, that he is most precious in the sight of God and is of the highest value in his service towards Him!**

Of interest, is the fact that when gold is super heated, it becomes translucent, just as the Bible describes the streets of Jerusalem to be. Furthermore, when gold is liquified, a blood colored sludge surfaces to the top. This intimates the blood covering of Jesus Christ, because of the crucible of the saint's walk of faith, on earth! Just as Shadrack, Mesheck and Abednego were tossed into the Babylonian furnace for their faith, whose temperature was super heated seven times above normal, the covering of the fourth man (Jesus Christ) provided deliverance from destruction, because the quality of their faith was also translucent! Therefore, this identifies and describes for us the fifth furnace of Righteous Judgment for The Church.

▶ **Furnace #6: The Furnace of Righteous Litigation**
2 Chronicles 28:3 AMP
"And he burned incense in the Valley of Ben-Hinnom [son of Hinnom] and burned his sons as an offering, after the abominable customs of the [heathen] nations whom the Lord drove out before the Israelites." (cf. Dan. 3:1-30; 1 Kgs. 11:1-10, 2 Kgs. 23:2-12)

Flies Are Drawn to Uncovered Food

The year was approximately 607 B.C. Israel was once again in Babylonian captivity. It seems that these Babylonians just won't go away! This fly won't buzz off, but wanders about a food source and that food item was Israel in Scripture, but also is humanity as a complete feast! Flies are drawn to uncovered food. Demonic spirits are also drawn to unprotected foodstuffs. I, for one, refuse to become or allow myself to be a food item on the table of the devil! Therefore, buzz off, in Jesus name!

2 Kings 23:10 AMP
"And Josiah defiled Topheth, which is in the Valley of Ben-hinnom [son of Hinnom], that no man might ever burn there his son or his daughter as an offering to Molech." (cf. Ezek. 16:21)

In this particular Scripture, the Babylonian fire god is identified with the name, Molech. It was to this god that human sacrifices were provided as fodder down through the centuries of human history of antiquity, from Nimrod to even in Daniel's day. But here in *2 Kings 23*, we find that pagan temples, idols and worship to Molech existed inside Jerusalem and in other provinces round about the city of David. Graveyards, containing the skeletal remains of children, were scattered even outside the gates and the walls of Jerusalem! The stench of death was all around! It's as if the slaughter house of Babylon obtained it's human livestock from the corral known as Jerusalem! It's as if this spider, called Babylon had deposited her eggs into the host body of Jerusalem as its prey, from which all her little hatchlings of carnality did spawn. In effect, these hatchlings cannibalized the host from within! *(cf. Jas. 3:14-4:2)*

Romans 6:11 AMP
"For sin, seizing the opportunity and getting a hold on me [by taking its incentive] from the commandment, beguiled and entrapped and cheated me and using it [as a weapon], killed me."

Nowadays, there are city and county ordinances that require bars, bath houses and liquor stores to maintain a minimum distance from any church. Depending on the region and zone, the distances may vary from three hundred to one thousand feet from any house of worship. But my question is, since when does distance or a particular locality make wickedness and pagan activity right or proper? It's the same as the brutal, husband or father who abuses his wife and children at home, but once out in public, that jerk becomes so pleasing and appealing to others. This man definitely deserves to be placed in the furnace of Righteous Litigation, wherein his carnality would be fuel for this iron apparatus of God. This then identifies and describes the sixth furnace called the Furnace of Righteous Litigation, for in it man's carnality is consumed through the due process of God's moral laws!

We Must Be Taught the Proper, Safe Use of Fire

Fire was used in animal sacrifices as unto the Lord for a sweet smelling savor. It seems that the Israelites had to be taught the proper use of fire. Imagine yourself, in the midst of Babylonian pagan worship on all sides. All you ever knew was what you observed or were taught according to the culture and custom. It would definitely effect your perception of life!

Just as God used a smoking furnace with Abram, it's possible that He used fire to teach the Hebrew nation, through Abraham, to overcome their fear of fire and how to use fire in worship to Him. After all, there is a correct way and a wrong way to use anything, especially fire. Because the Prophet Daniel, interpreted Nebuchadnezzar's dream, he was promoted to government positions along with his friends Shadrack, Mesheck and Abednego. *(cf. Dan. 2:47-49)* Approximately twenty years pass before Nebuchadnezzar built for himself an image, whose head was made of gold. *(cf. Dan. 3:1)* The king required that his officials, of whom Daniel and his friends were part, to gather together for the dedication and worship of this image. This decree conflicted with *Psalm 50:5* which states, "Gather together to Me My saints..." This proclamation also extended to the people, who occupied all other Babylonian provinces. *(cf. Dan. 3:2-4)*

Immediately, the king became enraged when Daniel's friends refused to comply with this royal edict. Being officials themselves, the king held them accountable, for they occupied higher official positions of integrity, loyalty and allegiance over and above those of lessor positions of authority. It was for this reason, I believe, that the king ordered the furnace to be heated seven times over for their incineration. The king perceived a threat and disloyalty. Any leader is held accountable, to maintain a higher level or standard of ethics than non leadership. Even a pagan fire worshiper knew that! But as a spiritual leader, the things of God must be rendered to Him and the things of men should be yielded to them. *(cf. Mat. 22:21)*

A Rolled Newspaper

Daniel's friends were eventually tightly bound and tossed in the furnace. *(cf. Dan. 3:15-27)* They were tightly bound head to foot, like a rolled newspaper. This technique ensured that they would burn slower than loose leaf paper, which would be immediately consumed in the flame. This tactic was meant to prolong their incineration. However, upon seeing a fourth man in the furnace, the king removed these intended human fire logs and promoted them once again! *(cf. Dan. 2:49, 3:30)*

When and wherever godly leadership exists, a higher standard of righteousness is always expected, recognized and honored. This recognition will set the same standard of righteousness for others to benefit by and to emulate, whether they are leadership or not. *(cf. Prov. 14:19, 29:2)*

Proverbs 11:10-11
"When it goeth well with the righteous, the city rejoices: and when the wicked perish, there is shouting. By the blessings of the upright the city is exalted: but it is overthrown by the mouth of the wicked."

▶ **Furnace #7: The Wrath of God's Righteous Judgment**
Revelation 1:14-15 AMP
"His head and His hair was like white wool, [as white] as snow, and His eyes [flashed] like a flame of fire [above]. His feet glowed like burnished (bright) bronze as it is refined in a furnace [below], and His voice was like the sound of many waters."

Revelation 14:8 AMP
"Then another angel, a second, followed, declaring, Fallen, fallen is Babylon the great! She who made all nations drink of the [maddening] wine of her passionate unchastity [idolatry]." (cf. Mat. 13:42, 50; Rev. 14:9-13)

Carnality to Burn

Isaiah 31:9b
"...Whose fire is in Zion and Whose furnace is in Jerusalem."

A flame above and a fire below! A demolition expert might say as a warning to others close by, "Fire in the hole!" but the Apostle

John described Jesus Christ as an eternal furnace of righteousness. The promise for each believer is to become as He is, as individual furnaces, wherein our carnality is to be burned by the all consuming fire of God! *(cf. 1 John 3:2)* Consider a chef who has a nice bird in the oven. Whether he dresses it or not does not matter. What does matter though, is that the bird is not over cooked and ruined. So the chef sets a watch on the bird, to ensure that the oven cooks the bird as intended. Well, God is as that chef! He watches that furnace to ensure that his people are not tormented in a flame, but are ready for service by the flame! The carnality within the blackened hole of the depths of our soul, is as fuel for the iron furnace in which to burn. In fact, God wants to place his iron furnace of righteous judgment deep within our soul, where carnality resides so that His fire would blaze away. Since the dross of one's carnality is the refuse of *his carnality, then the lamp of the wicked is that of a polluted flame. Like silver properties that turn yellow when exposed to light, the impure flame of carnality, becomes yellow as well. Therefore, this identifies and describes the seventh furnace to be the Furnace of God's Wrath and Righteous Judgment.* Truth #257: **Therefore, what a furnace is to liquefied metals, a kiln is to the progressive application of heat so as to bring the object inserted, to a mature strength and durability!**

Yellow is to Brass as Gold is to Faith

Man's carnality is the seed bed of all Babylonian tendencies. However, purified translucent faith is smokeless, for it is free of all carnal contaminants of unrighteousness. Yellow is a color of brass and gold is the color of faith! *Our misunderstanding of faith is also yellow, and like dross, it is an impurity of silver or lessor metals.* Did you know that there is a pure flame, which produces an invisible smoke. All you ever see is radiating heat as thermal waves above a sun baked object, such as the desert. Therefore, sunlight is a natural demonstration of pure faith, because there is no smoke just heat! On the other hand, colored smoke is the result of pollutants from a filthy flame or a fire base. And so it is with our carnality. Just as the burnt offerings of the Old Testament were as sweet smelling savors to God, likewise when the outgrowth of carnality is consumed within the soul of man, Almighty God is satisfied by the aroma of the death of His saints.

Closing Comments

God must purge each one of us by inserting us into the seven iron furnaces of earth, which are remedies for the sin element of our carnality. Mind you, I am not talking about one's reborn spirit. But I am identifying a problem area of the flesh, as it pertains to one's soul, which must be suppressed. God wants us to know that He will destroy the problem with the furnace of His wrath, if we fail to judge ourselves accordingly. He wants us to know that the problem is separate from us, individually. However, should we refuse to take the counter measures of righteous judgment to suppress our carnality, then mankind will force the hand of God, in that He will destroy the sin element first, but then destroy the sinner along with it, because as far as God is concerned, the problem and the sinner have become one. When we sow corruption in the flesh or allow it to remain, then we shall also reap the same corruption in the end! *(cf. 1 Cor. 15:50; Gal. 5:21; Col. 3:5-6; Rev. 14:12, 21:8, 27)*

This concludes the Old Testament saga or journey, an investigation of a lifestyle of repentance in FREEDOM I, FREEDOM II and FREEDOM III. In the months to come be sure to look for my continuing investigation of a lifestyle of repentance in the New Testament.

God bless you!

List of Axioms
Truths of Repentance
Freedom 1, II and III

▶ Truth #1: The call to repentance is a sound of alarm declaring you to change, while the call of repentance is a challenge to renew the spirit of your mind and then to change!

▶ Truth #2: If all we ever hear is repentance at the conversion level, for the sake of the sinner soon to be sainted, then the rest of the corporate Body of Christ suffers, as this will be all she will ever learn!

▶ Truth #3: A lifestyle of repentance is to agree with our adversary quickly, while we are in the way with him; lest at any time our adversary deliver us to the Judge, and the Judge deliver us to the officer and we be cast into prison!

▶ Truth #4: To self sentence one's self is to adopt a lifestyle of repentance!

▶ Truth #5: We cease from our striving by cutting, severing or removing ourselves from the source of misery or frustration or change the environment in which we may live or work!

▶ Truth #6: The place of repentance is intended to be within the soul of man; it is for this reason why Almighty God gave it to us!

▶ Truth #7: Whereas, the evidence [pollution] of the effects of man's carnality is clearly seen and known all around, it's only a reflection of the objective symptoms of man's wretchedness within!

▶ Truth #8: A lifestyle of repentance requires we possess a remorsefulness and a deep regret for all our carnality, so much so, that it grieves our heart!

▶ Truth #9: Therefore, a lifestyle of repentance is that corresponding action to faith, for it is a work of righteousness!

▶ Truth #10: First, a lifestyle of repentance will cause a pain of heart. Like a wound that has been exposed to iodine, or a transplanted tree that has experienced root shock, repentance will expose deep rooted carnality, as that residue of sin within the soul, for the entrance of God's Word brings light. Second, a lifestyle of repentance produces grief. This is not just to feel sorry for yourself, just because you were caught, but it intimates a genuine abhorrence for your carnality that still resides within. Third, a lifestyle of repentance means that God is permitted to direct whatever purging needs to be achieved and in whatever manner! Having met all three conditions, salvation is guaranteed, for in and through repentance, salvation is cultivated!

▶ Truth #11: Whereas, faith affords tangible cures, a lifestyle of repentance provides intangible remedies for the soul unto salvation! Whereas, faith is substance and evidence, repentance is the cleansing agent of the soul!

▶ **Truth #12:** Whereas, a confession of faith corresponds to our countenance, a lifestyle of repentance conforms to our carnality!

▶ **Truth #13:** A lifestyle of repentance mandates that everything about our lives agree with God's instructions of holiness and righteousness, because left to ourselves, man's goodness is always base and inferior in quality and content!

▶ **Truth #14:** A lifestyle of repentance then, is the manifestation of righteousness wherein, God's people are recipients of His favor and grace!

▶ **Truth #15:** A lifestyle of repentance serves as a memorial to the ever present carnality of man!

▶ **Truth #16:** A lifestyle of repentance means freedom; regret, based solely upon emotions, ulterior motives or convenience, means bondage again!

▶ **Truth #17:** So then, a true shriner is that saintly temple whose perfect heart is that secret dwelling place within his soul, and through a lifestyle of repentance, he has access to God, for without holiness, no man shall see God!

▶ **Truth #18:** A lifestyle of repentance is therefore, a curtain of God's sanctifying grace and the saints covering and consecration to God!

▶ **Truth #19:** Therefore, the knowledge of salvation facilitates

God's righteousness in and through a lifestyle of repentance!

▶ Truth #20: The revelation of the lifestyle of repentance is the light [knowledge] of salvation, for it qualifies faith!

▶ Truth #21: Since every saint is the temple [tabernacle] of the Holy Ghost, then each saint is also a priest of the Most High God and as priest, must wear the spiritual articles of the Urim and the Thummin upon his heart, because what the breastplate of judgment was to the Old Testament priest, the breastplate of righteousness is to the New Testament saint!

▶ Truth #22: False repentance means to possess a deep regret for a decision to be set free, based solely on external circumstances!

▶ Truth #23: Repentance should be a demonstrated way of life, for it is the knowledge of salvation that targets the way of righteousness, which is the true path of life!

▶ Truth #24: Since God repented of the evil which He thought to do against the people for their rebellion, shouldn't we repent also for our evil thoughts and intentions against one another, ahead of time, before it's too late?

▶ Truth #25: Repentance therefore, is retaining a meditation on the things of God, and having a remorse for all our iniquitous premeditation(s)!

▶ Truth #26: As any employee would receive a pay check for

his work as compensation, it is therefore common knowledge then, that there does exist a wage as a reward, for our carnality and a recompense for our respect to a lifestyle of repentance!

▶ Truth #27: Through a lifestyle of repentance, the saint touches God's soft spot!

▶ Truth #28: Through a lifestyle of repentance, the soul is afflicted even to the very depths of one's carnality!

▶ Truth #29: Through a lifestyle of repentance, the sacred cows of carnality are slaughtered as sin offerings of atonement for our ignorance!

▶ Truth #30: Through specific, working knowledge of the laws of faith and repentance, the saint exercises his legal right as a law abiding citizen of heaven!

▶ Truth #31: Just as the bull was killed at the altar of sacrifice, similarly, repentance for the saints of God, involves a killing! It requires the saints of God to die to the impulses of self gratification and to mortify their carnality, because the cross that most carry, is not the cross that they must carry!

▶ Truth #32: What the law of leprosy was to the disease, the law of repentance is to the residue of sin, our carnality; and what was symptomatic of leprosy to the people then, is indicative of the sin spores of carnality for people today!

▶ Truth #33: The reign of the inward work of God's righteousness upon the heart and soul of man is the effect of the law of repentance, because the reconciliation of his soul, as a living sacrifice, is the saint's reasonable service!

▶ Truth #34: Throughout life, the saint of God separates himself from all worldly distractions, either sensory or psychologically composing himself with the quiet preparations of his heart, because he knows that he must employ serious calculations of meekness to please his God!

▶ Truth #35: The saint's involvement is the atonement of his soul, because a lifestyle of repentance is the road less traveled! Therefore, the knowledge of the atoning work of Jesus Christ is the knowledge of salvation and repentance is that pathway of instruction in the way of righteousness!

▶ Truth #36: Just as the judge forces the issue of accountability to the offender, a lifestyle of repentance also forces the issue of carnality to the saint, for without repentance, he remains a fugitive!

▶ Truth #37: A lifestyle of repentance is most subjective, for it is the private examination and introspection of self as a cell within a box!

▶ Truth #38: Whereas, the brilliance of a diamond's fire is seen in its depth and cut, so too is the brilliance seen in the depth and cut of the saint's heart and soul, for he has become God's precious stone and in so doing, he is valuable!

▶ Truth #39: To bear the iniquity, means to be aware of the

smoking gun/relic that is of one's carnality and to consider its lethal effects upon the heart and soul!

▶ Truth #40: Whereas, a charge improves morale, repentance as a personal charge, enhances one's salvation!

▶ Truth #41: A lifestyle of repentance displaces complacency much like an object would displace water with its mass and volume, because the weight of a lifestyle of repentance pierces the depths of one's carnality!

▶ Truth #42: Christianity, a universal expression, does not absolve the saint of his duty to himself and of his obligation to God to repent, because a lifestyle of repentance is fatness to his soul!

▶ Truth #43: To remain unrepentant, means to be ignorant of our future!

▶ Truth #44: A lifestyle of repentance will draw God's good pleasure upon the saint!

▶ Truth #45: Through a lifestyle of repentance, the saint no longer allows himself to remain as table scraps, as that which is thrown to the dogs. Neither is he putting on the dog of religious dress up!

▶ Truth #46: A lifestyle of repentance sanitizes one's soul effectively removing the filth, refuse and droppings left behind by sin!

▶ **Truth #47:** Through a lifestyle of repentance, the saint relieves himself of all the pressures of his flesh. He is protected from exposure and vulnerability, because through his lifestyle of repentance, he minds his own business!

▶ **Truth #48:** Whereas, a shovel is for digging and covering, a lifestyle of repentance is the means of excavation for the soul in and through which carnality is exposed. Repentance is also a covering to bury that which is as waste matter of the carnal propensities!

▶ **Truth #49:** A lifestyle of repentance is the shovel long since neglected by the church, for the church fails to realize her need for this shovel called repentance!

▶ **Truth #50:** Whereas, physical strength is external and is often an audacious display of vanity, moral strength is that of the heart, for it is the internal function of holiness!

▶ **Truth #51:** Repentance is a spiritual tool which the saint uses and the Holy Ghost employs to dig up, scoop away, turn over, bury, trench and grade the residue of sin within his soul!

▶ **Truth #52:** The shovel of repentance is the tool by which carnality is expunged from the soul and by which salvation is cultivated in the heart!

▶ **Truth #53:** The reason that carnality exist, is to reveal the need/purpose for repentance!

▶ Truth #54: Through a lifestyle of repentance, the little child called carnality, is found out and punished, for it is the accursed thing!

▶ Truth #55: Through a lifestyle of repentance, God's wrath is stayed, because the saint has acquired carnal knowledge by which he is able to suppress the insurgency within his soul!

▶ Truth #56: Through a lifestyle of repentance, the saint unearths his carnality, and as an act of discovery, reveals that which is holy before the Lord and destroys the accursed carnality within him!

▶ Truth #57: Repentance then, is a personal assessment of the saint's obedience to the word of faith and to the word of God's righteousness!

▶ Truth #58: Without the knowledge of salvation, as carnal knowledge, a lifestyle of repentance is a waste of time!

▶ Truth #59: Through a lifestyle of repentance, the saint deals with the carnal problem first, but has compassion for the person. Repentance therefore, involves the restoration of one's position and possession!

▶ Truth #60: A lifestyle of repentance involves the adopted method of the operation of God's righteousness at work within the soul, for it is a life long journey to discipline the soul against carnality!

▶ **Truth #61:** Through a lifestyle of repentance, the saint like a parent, trains the little child within his soul, whose name is carnality, to behave!

▶ **Truth #62:** Man's carnality is that little child within his soul, and must be disciplined and suppressed!

▶ **Truth #63:** Through a lifestyle of repentance, the saint brings forth fruits of repentance, as he redeems his soul from the ravages of his carnality!

▶ **Truth #64:** A lifestyle of repentance is therefore, progenitive in that regeneration, reconstruction, reformation and reconciliation of the saint's condition, in his carnality has begun, for he has positioned himself to be a recipient of Christ's redemption!

▶ **Truth #65:** A lifestyle of repentance means that the saint must wear the mantle of repentance over a cloak of humility!

▶ **Truth #66:** A lifestyle of repentance is as a switchback, for its many turns to the saint's carnal mind, and its evidence is seen as the standard of righteousness that is raised against carnal devices!

▶ **Truth #67:** A lifestyle of repentance is the ongoing activity of taking the proper assessment of life by keeping first things first, between creature comforts and spiritual integrity!

▶ **Truth #68:** Through a lifestyle of repentance, the saint acknowledges his character flaws as he judges his smitten hear of its foolhardiness!

▶ Truth #69: Merely stating, "I repent" or to follow the instructions from a pulpit without a cost factor involved negates true, godly repentance, because it is evangelical in scope. However, through a lifestyle of repentance, the saint makes provision for the renewal of the spirit of his mind and the regeneration of his soul, by taking special pains to cater his heart to God!

▶ Truth #70: All commitments to a lifestyle of repentance involves our mutual participation, because repentance activates the atoning power found in the blood!

▶ Truth #71: Repentance then, is recognizing Jesus Christ as the lobbyist who paid His own price to maintain our cause!

▶ Truth #72: Repentance then is a cause and a pursuit of a mission in and throughout life. Repentance is a cause for battle, and as an entreaty, this lifestyle calls upon God to maintain our cause. Repentance gives strength for the battle, because repentance is an assurance of victory and strength for the battles of life!

▶ Truth #73: Through a lifestyle of repentance, the saint will no longer compartmentalize his relationship with God, separating or excluding the workings of God's righteousness from his daily living!

▶ Truth #74: Through a lifestyle of repentance, the saint offers a just wage as a spiritual judgment against his carnality!

▶ **Truth #75:** Through a lifestyle of repentance, the saint exercises his spiritual right to enforce his "Victim's Bill of Rights" demanding restitution specifically, for the return of lost or stolen property, lost territory and lost positions!

▶ **Truth #76:** Through a lifestyle of repentance, the saint of God seeks spiritual asylum! He becomes an apostate to the things of this world, because he has decided to reject that which has been familiar to the things of his own carnality!

▶ **Truth #77:** For the saint, the altar of asylum is a lifestyle of repentance, for it enriches and fortifies his faith in Jesus Christ, Who is his redeemer, his Refuge, and his Fortress against the self indulgences of his carnality and the stratagems of this fallen world! Through repentance, the saints of God obtain sanctuary with impunity!

▶ **Truth #78:** Whereas, carnality is as putting on the dog, in that people doggedly choose to do so, likewise the pony refers to the mulishness [mule headed] of the progenitors of a sugarcoated, convenient faith, for without repentance as a corresponding action, this kind of faith alone, is a circus act!

▶ **Truth #79:** Without repentance as the knowledge of salvation, people perish as the collateral damage caused by carnality!

▶ **Truth #80:** Through a lifestyle of repentance, the saint has boldness to lay out the criteria for God's blessings, which are His provisions for triumphant living and a victorious life in Christ!

▶ **Truth #81:** Through a lifestyle of repentance, the saint retains his integrity before the Lord his God!

▶ **Truth #82:** When a saint sets his heart to seek after God's righteousness, through a lifestyle of repentance, entire communities, cities and nations may be brought back into right standing with Almighty God!

▶ **Truth #83:** What the feast days are to ceremonies commemorating historical fact, a lifestyle of repentance on the other hand, is the saint's solemn and sober assessment and examination of his heart!

▶ **Truth #84:** Through a lifestyle of repentance, the saint chastens himself before the Lord his God, declaring his need for divine intervention against the carnal dysfunctions within his soul!

▶ **Truth #85:** Through a lifestyle of repentance, age is never a factor, only the heart of one who seeks the Lord, as a deer that pants after the water brook does!

▶ **Truth #86:** A lifestyle of repentance is therefore an appointed, authoritative determination against the carnality within the soul, thereby making the saint a choice selection, because of his respect for the recompense for the reward!

▶ **Truth #87:** Through a lifestyle of repentance, our smitten heart motivates and agitates our soul to travail for the carnality that has crept in and over the walls that have fallen, thereby rendering the saint a victim or a prey!

▶ **Truth #88:** A lifestyle of repentance represents a due diligence and a vigilance towards this end, to audaciously rebuild one's character of godliness by living uprightly before God and men!

▶ **Truth #89:** The gift of repentances given to the saints of God, for such a time as this!

▶ **Truth #90:** A lifestyle of repentance then, is the intimacy of an intercourse, because the saint stands in the inner court and in the very presence of God!

▶ **Truth #91:** A lifestyle of repentance is a writ of habeas corpus, since the saint declares his presence in his house of reply, because he has honored the summons of his Judge, Almighty God, Himself!

▶ **Truth #92:** Like Job, a lifestyle of repentance forces introspection, because the saint has declared himself before God. He has brought his body according to God's demand to be a living sacrifice, lest a bench warrant be issued for his arrest by the Judge of all creation!

▶ **Truth #93:** A lifestyle of repentance then, is a sacrifice in righteousness unto Almighty God, for it is always founded upon faith in Jesus Christ!

▶ **Truth #94:** A lifestyle of repentance provides a recommitment to our duty, as law abiding citizens, before Almighty God!

▶ Truth #95: Repentance is a consecrating gift of God's grace to carnal men!

▶ Truth #96: Like David, whenever the saint sins greatly, as all of us have at one time or another, to avoid such a trap again, a lifestyle of repentance often prevents us from repeating the same transgression, but also the saint shall never forget the circumstances involved or the ramifications it caused!

▶ Truth #97: Through a lifestyle of repentance, the saint avoids the paranoia of personal destruction!

▶ Truth #98: A lifestyle of repentance thwarts the difficulties of life. Although the difficulties may arise, the saint of God is not ravaged by them!

▶ Truth #99: A lifestyle of repentance is keeping one's distance away from sin. The saint of God seeks the good and hates the evil!

▶ Truth #100: Through a lifestyle of repentance, the absolution obtained is the remission given for amnesty!

▶ Truth #101: Through a lifestyle of repentance, the saint repossesses his emotional, mental and spiritual constitution as he redirects his anger, anxieties and frustrations to a positive and a constructive conclusion and not to a destructive or a negative end!

▶ Truth #102: The Holy Spirit's reproof is an integral element in true godly repentance!

▶ Truth #103: Without the Holy Spirit, mere lip service on our part, renders repentance ineffective and suspect as well!

▶ Truth #104: A lifestyle of repentance leads the saint into godly instruction!

▶ Truth #105: Through a lifestyle of repentance, God permits a thorn in the flesh to keep the saint penitent, for repentance is a memorial to the carnality within the soul of men!

▶ Truth #106: Through a lifestyle of repentance, the saint reasons with Almighty God as He presents His argument against carnality. The saint doesn't debate, haggle or strive with God, for he knows that God has all the facts about his carnality, where the saint does not!

▶ Truth #107: Through a lifestyle of repentance, the Holy Ghost shall cause the saint to know wisdom and instruct him in it so that he may spiritually perceive, with skill and cunning, God's words with understanding, enabling him to comprehend the way of righteousness!

▶ Truth #108: Through a lifestyle of repentance, a man remains righteous for he stands in his uprightness before God, because he judges himself and in doing so, he retains that quality of holiness as unto the Lord!

▶ Truth #109: Through a lifestyle of repentance, the righteous of God will not patronize the local taverns of worldliness to consume the spirits therein, because Almighty God commands His people to assimilate the secrets of His kingdom, which He has placed within them!

▶ Truth #110: Through a lifestyle of repentance, the saint exhibits the objective symptoms of righteousness, because his uprightness is the evidence of the covering of God's righteousness over him!

▶ Truth #111: So then to be filled, is a progression and a pursuit of a righteous character, for godliness is spiritual training!

▶ Truth #112: Whereas, God has reconciled all things unto Himself, and this includes the saint's reborn spirit, He has also left His saint with the cause of the reconciliation of his soul. Therefore, what God's righteousness is to His judgment, reconcile is to the restoration of all things, and what the saint's righteousness is to his training in godliness, the ministry of reconciliation is to the suppression of the saint's carnality!

▶ Truth #113: Therefore, since the law of the land establishes a basis for conduct and behavior as law abiding, so too then, does the word of God's righteousness legislate a standard of upright conduct and behavior for the saint!

▶ Truth #114: Through His righteous judgment, Almighty God has already judged the offense of man's self righteousness and the injury it has become to the universe. Therefore, God's judgment for the eternal good of the universe, as an end to itself, is the final decision for the soul of man, but against his carnality! The intended result being, that the soul of man would be saved and the universe preserved.

▶ Truth #115: Therefore, the purpose of God's righteousness is the judgment of an unrighteous world, and the reason for righteousness is that the saint would judge that which evinces the symptoms of his self righteousness, as a condition for the sentence! It is cause and effect, because the causative factor of self righteousness is the carnality of an impenitent heart, and the effect of impenitence, is the eternal damnation of an unrepentant soul!

▶ Truth #116: The saint of God cannot have genuine peace with God unless he embraces a lifestyle of repentance, which is altogether righteousness!

▶ Truth #117: Whereas the produce of fruit and vegetables which are harvested and made available for the picking by the consumer, the fruit of righteousness will likewise make the saint, as the elect of God, the salt of the earth and the pick of the bunch, because his character demands attention!

▶ Truth #118: As a first principle of repentance, any sacrifice of righteousness must involve the self examination of motives, the end result of which would be turning from that which is selfishness!

▶ Truth #119: Whereas, righteousness, as a close order discipline is a cause for the saint, godliness is the effect and therefore the demonstration of God's righteousness upon the saint!

▶ Truth #120: Repentance is a judgment against carnality, thereby disturbing it and frustrating the saint to be attentive to the undisciplined recruit that is within his soul!

▶ Truth #121: Through a lifestyle of repentance, the saint of God is very subjective about his own carnality; thus, he recognizes the objective symptoms of self righteousness in those about him!

▶ Truth #122: Therefore, what the book of Ecclesiastes is to man's carnality, Ekklesia is to the carnality in and of the churches. And what the remnant of God is to the called out ones, the prefix, Ek are to those saints who have separated themselves, from others who remain carnal, and have sanctified themselves by exposing their own carnality!

▶ Truth #123: Like the shiftless inmate, who allows time served to become his enemy, the man who fails to reconcile his heart to God, shall also continue in his carnality!

▶ Truth #124: Through a lifestyle of repentance, the saint conforms himself to God's word, because he chooses, as a function of his will, to persevere in holiness for the rest of his life! In other words, there's no doubt about it!

▶ Truth #125: Through a lifestyle of repentance, in choosing to be obedient to the moral laws of God, the saint would be in authority over his carnal cravings, but also his choice would be virtuous, because his choice to obey the word of God, in the conformity of his heart and life to all known and practical truths, would be the conditions and the means of the highest good of being!

▶ Truth #126: Just as the Prophet Jonah was cast into the deep, Almighty God commands us to cast ourselves out into the deep, for only those who do so shall behold the works of God within their souls and they shall see His wonders in the depths of their carnality!

▶ Truth #127: Like a body that has been tethered to a block of concrete and has sunk to the ocean's floor, carnality is that which Satan has fastened to the floor of one's soul!

► Truth #128: When a man develops a lifestyle of repentance, he has truly received a blessing from above, for he has acknowledged his carnality, and in this, he is a recipient of the blessings from the deep!

► Truth #129: Therefore, what a gauge is to a vehicle's instrumentation, the gage of obligation is to the challenge of regeneration and renewal!

► Truth #130: Through a lifestyle of repentance, the saint, as an act of his will, chooses to recognize carnal propensities, because repentance is the process of forsaking selfishness, thereby saving his soul! Because the saint has come to reason with Almighty God, he agrees with God's argument against him!

► Truth #131: Whereas, the force of gravity is a natural law of creation which draws, voluntariness on the other hand, is a force of unreasonableness, because selfishness gravitates towards self gratification!

► Truth #132: Through a lifestyle of repentance, a saint reasons with Almighty God, and as he does so, he clarifies what he thinks he knows by suppressing his carnality, his selfishness, his bias and short sightedness to reveal what he really doesn't know. What is left is the truth that he should know, and it is this truth that will set him free!

► Truth #133: A lifestyle of repentance is an accomplishment done as a condition of IF or MIGHT, which transfigures a saint consecrated, and whose aim is to be sanctified!

► Truth #134: Whereas, even the healthiest person would not be able to fully purge his body of these parasites, likewise man will never purge his soul of his carnality! Just as a built up immune system suppresses the rampant out growth of these internal parasites, likewise, a lifestyle of repentance suppresses carnality, which is that parasite of the soul!

▶ Truth #135: Whereas, the kiln requires time to bake the object inserted into it, likewise a lifestyle of repentance requires a lifetime to process God's righteousness into the heart and soul of that saint!

▶ Truth #136: The kiln of repentance is as a furnace in which the contaminate, called carnality, is extracted from the soul. The brazen heart is made fluid, because the saint, as brass, has willingly surrendered his soul, thereby forging his salvation!

▶ Truth #137: Through a lifestyle of repentance, self righteousness leaves a bitter taste in the saint's mouth!

▶ Truth #138: Through a lifestyle of repentance, the saint responds to God's demand as his obligation, which necessitates his justification!

▶ Truth #139: A lifestyle of repentance is that which is trouble to resurgent carnality, because it is the agitation exerted to mortify selfish propensities!

▶ Truth #140: Through a lifestyle of repentance, the saint trembles at the very thought of carnal resurgence, because the truth of God's Word has impacted his heart so much so, that he has become a recipient of God's power coursing through him as a current would through a high power cable!

▶ Truth #141: A lifestyle of repentance represents an exposed soul, for repentance enables the saint to strip himself of all that is carnal and that is a reproach to God, because man's carnality is his shame!

▶ Truth #142: Carnality, in the fashion of will worship is only an external, mechanical expression. It is just a public display and evinces self exaltation. True repentance however, is an intimate and private preparation. In this, the saint's private preparation of a penitent heart is displayed, because private practice begets public performance!

▶ Truth #143: Through a lifestyle of repentance, the saint removes his name from the book of rebellion, and transfers it, as a new name written down in the book of remembrance as well as in the book of life, because his intelligent, active faith has enabled the saint to overcome this unrighteous world!

▶ Truth #144: Whereas, the earth is celestial within the solar system, the face of the world is unrighteous in the fashion of man's carnality!

▶ Truth #145: Through a lifestyle of repentance, godliness is the main attraction and as such the saint, whose character is righteous, shall be judged accordingly!

▶ Truth #146: When a man refuses to develop his character in God while he lives, that man by default, allows himself to become effeminate due to the whoredom of his spiritual adultery [carnality]!

▶ Truth #147: As long as a man refuses to repent, he exalts his whoredoms transcending God, because he gives his carnality the prominence above God!

▶ Truth #148: Impenitent humanity remains rebellious and therefore self righteous, because people refuse to repent of their selfishness!

▶ Truth #149: Since man is a biped being, he was created to walk [uprightly]. Therefore, he was created to exalt the Lord God, his creator in his uprightness!

▶ Truth #150: Therefore, the saint's scrutiny of his own carnality through a lifestyle of repentance, is a spiritual discipline in which righteousness, holiness and sanctification are godly features plotted across the landscape of his soul!

▶ Truth #151: A lifestyle of repentance, is the investigation of one's carnality, for carnality exists within the soul. It is an evil entity which must be plotted and charted as an illusive enemy within a person's psyche!

▶ Truth #152: The impenitent have as their lobbyist Satan, for he is the accuser of the brethren as well as the father of all sinners. Therefore, because they are in league with him, Satan stands in proxy against them!

▶ Truth #153: A lifestyle of repentance is a cause for Christ, because righteousness is a ministry of the soul's reconciliation, which Jesus Christ presents before the court of God on behalf of every saint!

▶ Truth #154: Through a lifestyle of repentance, the saint of God acquires understanding of the knowledge of salvation, because he ash been enlightened by the Spirit of wisdom and of revelation!

▶ Truth #155: Therefore, to be truly cool in this life, one must walk uprightly before Almighty God in uprightness, forsaking self righteousness!

▶ Truth #156: Through a lifestyle of repentance, the saint becomes a prisoner of Jesus Christ, because he has reconciled his soul according to the light of God's Word of truth. His goodness then, is the saint's justification and qualification as a citizen of heaven's prism, the new city of Jerusalem, coming down, because there is restricted air space reserved for those who have served Him!

▶ Truth #157: A lifestyle of repentance requires that the saint come to grip with his own carnality, and that he know that any association with the dictates of his selfish propensities is a very big deal to God!

▶ Truth #158: A lifestyle of repentance is not a sham or a burlesque, as a mockery of pure, undefiled religion. It is however, the employment of truth upon a cheating carnal heart!

▶ Truth #159: Repentance means that the saint will no longer coddle, rationalize or justify his carnality!

▶ Truth #160: The justification of carnality is the rationalization that everything is well and that there are no absolutes, because the carnal propensity is a pimp to the motivation of convenience and obsessive compulsiveness!

▶ Truth #161: Altogether, a lifestyle of repentance is the accumulation of the knowledge of salvation, as the instructions in righteousness. It is also the knowledge of carnality, which is akin to godliness and sanctification, because of its exposure to the light!

▶ Truth #162: Through a lifestyle of repentance, the saint will cast down his iniquity and confess his carnality. In this, his character of godliness is developed, because he has brought every thought into the obedience of Christ!

▶ Truth #163: Through a lifestyle of repentance, the saint will no longer treat God false heartedly, as a wife who has departed from her husband, for he has purposed in his heart to live uprightly before Him!

▶ Truth #164: A sinner is not a sinner merely because he is a non believer. He is a sinner because he rejects the truth of God's Word and is therefore in a state or position of being an apostate! This also applies to the ungodly, those who were once godly but have since fallen away or have backslided!

▶ Truth #165: Repentance then, is the moderate wind of righteous judgment against carnality [moral depravity, selfishness, sin], for without this wind of the saint's judgment [propitiation] of his own carnality, how shall his carnal soul be cleansed?

▶ Truth #166: A lifestyle of repentance is as the thermal wind of righteous judgment, which the saint blows against the stubble of his carnality that stretches across the wilderness of his parched soul, which has been deprived of the moisture of God's Word!

▶ Truth #167: Due to a prevailing physical condition, a heart murmur is an undesirable noise within the heart, and so it is within God's heart. Due to a prevailing human condition, impenitent humanity is the murmur of His heart!

▶ Truth #168: A lifestyle of repentance engages the travail of the soul, which the saint must allow and execute to relieve the pressures of his carnality, for travail is the process of elimination!

▶ Truth #169: A lifestyle of repentance involves an excavation to till the fallow ground, uprooting the stubble of carnality!

▶ Truth #170: Just as the curing of concrete would involve the regulation of humidity and temperature, likewise, the germination process of the seed also involves the regulation of moisture and climate. Therefore, the fallow ground of a hardened heart must be tilled and then prepared to receive the seed of God's Word, if carnality is ever to be suppressed and the soul is to regenerated!

▶ Truth #171: The saint plants seeds of repentance in the vineyard of his heart, because repentance causes him to be planted, and if planted in God, then the saint shall eventually be built up and then translated!

▶ Truth #172: A lifestyle of repentance requires the saint to pioneer his own recovery from his carnality, by suppressing it and tearing out the defiled heart with violence!

▶ Truth #173: A lifestyle of repentance cancels God's judgment against us. Impenitence ushers it in upon us, for we have condemned ourselves to it because faith has been broken and righteousness has been spurned!

▶ Truth #174: A lifestyle of repentance then, is the method of sculpting righteousness as by the finger prints of God, through the application of righteous judgment against carnality!

▶ Truth #175: Through a lifestyle of repentance, the saint of God becomes a terror to his carnal self, which means that he has conscripted God's righteous judgment against his own carnality!

▶ Truth #176: Therefore, to become a subscriber of God's promises necessitates that humanity obey the commandments of righteousness! Otherwise, impenitent humanity shall not receive the righteous promises of God!

▶ Truth #177: Through a lifestyle of repentance, the saint remains acceptable in God's sight, for he has amended his ways, and has developed the necessary spiritual disciplines by the restorative application of righteousness against his carnality, which assists him in his triumph over moral depravities with the specific knowledge of salvation!

▶ Truth #178: Applying this definition to repentance, then it could be said, What a lifestyle of repentance is to the doctrine of God, philosophy is to the knowledge of salvation, for without this knowledge, how could salvation be cultivated?

▶ Truth #179: It is therefore evident, that God's word of righteousness possesses a duplicity of judgment against carnality and of the fulfillment of His promises, thereby making God's promises equivalent to His commands!

▶ Truth #180: There is no other alternative for the Body of Christ, but for the church to abhor the carnality within!

▶ Truth #181: Repentance is not a temporary antidote for a permanent carnal problem. Rather, a lifestyle of repentance is God's righteous remedy for man's carnal tragedy!

▶ Truth #182: Those who are derelict with the application of the measuring line of righteous judgment against their carnality, are also in neglect of the measure of faith! Therefore, Almighty God must exact judgment against impenitent humanity for this abuse!

▶ Truth #183: A lifestyle of repentance is as a vertical line of judgment against carnality, for it enables the saint to retain his righteous integrity between God and himself!

▶ Truth #184: What God's mercy is to His pardon, His grace is to His provision!

▶ Truth #185: Through a lifestyle of repentance, the saint becomes God's remnant. The reformation of our ways and of our doings is of higher call, in that such conduct and behavior is visible to God, but also by others in and through our godly character!

▶ Truth #186: Therefore, Jesus Christ lived a lifestyle of repentance. What's more, the content of His character is the fruit of the Spirit which is righteousness, peace and joy in the Holy Ghost!

▶ Truth #187: A lifestyle of repentance stops the emaciation process and restores wholeness, health and well being. In this, the Lord God takes pleasure in the death of His saints!

▶ Truth #188: Whereas, anything consumed or is ingested may either defile or enhance one's anatomy, likewise that which is sensually assimilated may also pollute or cleanse the soul by arousing carnality or spirituality; for the kingdom of God is not in food or drink only, but it is righteousness, peace and joy in the Holy Ghost!

▶ Truth #189: Through a lifestyle of repentance, the soul remains undefiled and the saint stays reconciled to God, through the ministry of reconciliation which Almighty God has given him!

▶ Truth #190: The reality of a lifestyle of repentance, provides longevity of life as it prevails over man's carnality, because repentance keeps the beast in its cage!

▶ Truth #191: Through a lifestyle of repentance, the saint suppresses his carnality and he purifies his mind of iniquitous thoughts!

▶ Truth #192: Whereas, any pet should be trained to obey, likewise, carnal man must also attend obedience school to suppress his carnal tendencies. He does so through a lifestyle of repentance, which is his obedience to the instructions in righteousness!

▶ Truth #193: Spiritual adultery is the diametric condition to righteousness and is therefore a lifestyle of carnality, which embraces idolatry and suckles that which is morally depraved!

▶ Truth #194: Through a lifestyle of repentance, the saint impregnates his soul with the richness that is of God, through faith is Christ alone, thereby propagating his salvation as a son of God!

▶ Truth #195: Without a lifestyle of repentance, we waste ourselves, because we sentence ourselves to eternal death!

▶ Truth #196: Without a lifestyle of repentance, a man confirms his divorce and estrangement from God, because his decree of unfaithfulness to his moral obligation to be righteous, has been predetermined through the choices of the individual!

▶ Truth #197: What sanctification is to the saints separation from the things of this world, carnality is to the self righteous, as a separation from the things of God!

▶ Truth #198: An obvious character trait of the impenitent and the carnally minded is their refusal to have anything to do with that which contradicts their tradition and challenges their carnality!

▶ Truth #199: Without a lifestyle of repentance, denial is to be expected by those who resist the truth of the gospel. Their denial intimates an alternative mind set which negates reality, whether spiritual or physical, for they possess ulterior motives!

▶ Truth #200: The saint seeks after righteousness through a lifestyle of repentance because repentance is a moral obligation to God, himself and others as a spiritual discipline of that which ought to be done!

▶ Truth #201: A lifestyle of repentance then is the ground for the obligation as a consideration for salvation which ought to be inherently desired, for God has placed that longing in the heart of every man. Therefore, a lifestyle of repentance is that duty of oughtness, which is that which ought to be done, to achieve the highest good, namely salvation!

▶ **Truth #202:** Without a lifestyle of repentance, a person dispossesses himself of the provisions of His salvation which were given to him on the cross at Calvary. With repentance however, the saint retains his salvation and his resurrection shall be the evidence of his reward!

▶ **Truth #203:** The battlefield is our soul. The objective then, is to suppress carnality and the tour of duty is our entire life! Through a lifestyle of repentance, the saint engages in spiritual warfare employing spiritual weaponry and battle tactics to lacerate, shatter, rend and tear his carnality and his entrenched strongholds!

▶ **Truth #204:** Through a lifestyle of repentance, the saint remembers that he is not his own and that Almighty God holds the title deed on his life and all his material possessions!

▶ **Truth #205:** A lifestyle of repentance is a spiritual discipline undertaken by those saints of God, who are of a violent disposition and who possess a righteous indignation against their own carnality! A passive, cursive and effortless pretense of repentance will be of no benefit, because a lifestyle of repentance is a duty and this makes it an obligation for the highest good or end, namely the salvation of the soul!

▶ **Truth #206:** The friction caused by the shearing stress of carnality against the intended order of righteousness is eliminated through a lifestyle of repentance!

▶ **Truth #207:** Holiness clothing is an external deviate dress code, to that which is flesh and temporal. Since no man is to know another according to the flesh, it is reasonable to reject such nonsensical postulations of disturbed men!

▶ **Truth #208:** Through a lifestyle of repentance, the methods applied to binding and loosing may be summed up in just one simple technique. Simply put, the saint binds the spirit of his mind to the Spirit of the Mind of Christ. As he loosens the carnal penchants of the spirit of his carnal mind, he also loosens the charges that are his in and through the Mind of Christ!

▶ **Truth #209:** Just as a movie director would create an environment that liberates the actor to express himself freely, likewise the environment created through faith and repentance, which the saint creates for himself, liberates the Holy Ghost within him to express Himself through the saint, as He is God's mouthpiece!

▶ **Truth #210:** A man lacking godliness, sits back bolted to the framework of his carnality and intentionally watches and purposely allows all manner of influences free passage into his heart, his home and his society!

▶ **Truth #211:** A lifestyle of repentance establishes righteous judgment against carnality within the gates of the theater of the mind, thereby undergirding the branches of the heart and soul with faith quality decisions. Consequently, repentance possesses a lawfulness as a decision from the executive faculty of the will, as a resolute judgment made for the soul and against carnality within it!

▶ **Truth #212:** A lifestyle of repentance, postpones God's judgment!

▶ **Truth #213:** Repentance then is to seek divine litigation as prosecution to mitigate [suppress] carnality that we might live!

▶ Truth #214: A lifestyle of repentance is like trampling grapes, because the saint marks time in place contemplating his life and scrutinizing his carnality!

▶ Truth #215: Therefore, a lifestyle of repentance is the pressing force that crushes the sour grapes of one's carnality, so that the saint will not be lost in the sea of forgetfulness or perish in the lake of fire!

▶ Truth #216: Through a lifestyle of repentance, the saint grieves not the Holy Ghost, because he has been sealed unto the day of redemption, since he willingly rends his heart on behalf of others!

▶ Truth #217: Through a lifestyle of repentance, the saint willingly places himself in harm's way, so that he may deprive his carnality of its self indulgences. In doing so, he recovers that which was once dead within him, because he has a nose for it!

▶ Truth #218: Therefore, in faith and through a lifestyle of repentance, the saint is sealed because he obeys God's Word, complies to His will and conforms his life to God's ways!

▶ Truth #219: A lifestyle of repentance is the saint's intercession and petition. It is therefore his litigation, as a request for a stay of execution!

▶ Truth #220: Through a lifestyle of repentance, the saint becomes very much aware of his mortality and his vulnerability!

▶ Truth #221: A lifestyle of repentance then, is a work of righteousness and is therefore a walk of faith to execute judgment upon our own carnality!

▶ **Truth #222:** A lifestyle of repentance then is a counter measure against the corruption of this world and within ourselves. Therefore, righteousness like salt, is the preservative of the saint's virtue of holiness!

▶ **Truth #223:** A lifestyle of repentance denotes that the saint possesses an understanding of the knowledge of salvation and that he teach repentance to his posterity!

▶ **Truth #224:** Through a lifestyle of repentance, a contrite spirit, and a broken, penitent heart will attract God's favor and His regard shall be upon that saint whose heart is remorseful for the ascent of his carnality, and who is truly humble and thoroughly penitent before the Lord his God!

▶ **Truth #225:** Through a lifestyle of repentance, the saint is vomited from his deep bondage, because he has acknowledged the truth!

▶ **Truth #226:** Through a lifestyle of repentance, the saint protects the color of his heart's complexion, because repentance maintains his godly character!

▶ **Truth #227:** Since these twisted roots took their shape and were planted into my soul by events, situations and seasons of circumstance, so too must they be uprooted by events, situations and seasons of circumstance that are just as forceful and deep reaching, thereby cancelling out the negative with a positive!

▶ **Truth #228:** Through a lifestyle of repentance, any bondage shall vomit the saint, because he has allowed himself to feel a pain which God wanted him to feel; and the Word of

God is the potting soil, by which the saint has transplanted his heart in righteousness!

▶ Truth #229: Moreover, just as any mountain climber would vomit due to the extreme altitudes he has exposed himself too; likewise, a lifestyle of repentance will cause the saint to be vomited, and like any regurgitation, it hurts!

▶ Truth #230: Through a lifestyle of repentance, we get our priorities straight in that we place the value of souls above the material things in our life. In doing so, the saint guards himself against the gourds in his life!

▶ Truth #231: Through a lifestyle of repentance, the saint considers his ways, thereby establishing the Word of God's righteousness in his own heart!

▶ Truth #232: Baldness represents a lifestyle of repentance, for it is something that the saint must do to shave the continual growth of his carnality!

▶ Truth #233: A lifestyle of repentance is a precedent that precedes righteous judgment, because man's premise of God's loving kindness and mercy are the basis for His argument against man's carnality, apologetically speaking!

▶ Truth #234: Like the rod that is used for the back of fools, so too is righteous judgment the utensil that is applied to the hearts of impenitent men!

▶ Truth #235: A lifestyle of repentance sets the standard upon the unrighteous, because the remnant of God are His preachers of righteousness to an unrighteous world, in and through their lifestyle of repentance!

▶ Truth #236: A lifestyle of repentance is a lifelong, forensic investigative process of self examination!

▶ Truth #237: The time for repentance is a time of refreshing, for the penitent saint seeks righteousness and because he does so, he shall be concealed in the day of God's wrath upon this unrighteous world, primarily because he won't be here!

▶ Truth #238: Therefore, a lifestyle of repentance is as an emollient oil, which lubricates the wheel of the cycle of grace upon any land, nation and people!

▶ Truth #239: Therefore, what rehabilitation may be to an inmates restoration, reconciliation is to the saint's transformation from his carnality to spiritual maturity!

▶ Truth #240: A lifestyle of repentance is a pursuit of righteousness, which produces peace; whereas, a lollygagging church is symptomatic of a careless, spiritual refrain! Through repentance then, any carnal restraint is an effect of righteousness unto godliness and peace!

▶ Truth #241: A lifestyle of repentance is necessary to counteract the passivity of one's carnality!

▶ Truth #242: Through a lifestyle of repentance, the righteous bruise which Jesus Christ received on our behalf, supplants the carnal bruise which Satan applied to the soul of man, as a brand of his usurpation against the authority of Almighty God!

▶ **Truth #243:** Through a lifestyle of repentance, the saint does consider his carnal ways of self indulgence. In doing so, he makes a faith quality decision to live righteously, actively building upon the foundation of God's Word!

▶ **Truth #244:** A lifestyle of repentance provides the saint of God the constructive activity which is conducive to righteousness! In this, he shall not dawdle aimlessly about or loiter at the cross!

▶ **Truth #245:** A lifestyle of repentance reanimates the saint's heart taking aim, focus and alignment at essential and pertinent matters of spiritual significance!

▶ **Truth #246:** Through a lifestyle of repentance, a saint builds his life upon the firm foundation of the prophets and of God's Word in three distinct ways, which are the Living Word, the Written Word and the Revealed Word!

▶ **Truth #247:** A lifestyle of repentance is a right of passage from the old, stale traditions of our carnality to new transitions of godliness!

▶ **Truth #248:** A lifestyle of repentance is an exhibition of our love for our enemies and their damned souls!

▶ **Truth #249:** Through a lifestyle of repentance, the saint keeps the charge of his sanctuary!

▶ **Truth #250:** Through a lifestyle of repentance, the priestly saint heeds God's pangs of death to repent, because they are stiff warnings from God that must not be ignored!

▶ Truth #251: Through a lifestyle of repentance, the bondage of fear and torment caused by past experiences, are replaced with a healthy understanding of the fear of the Lord!

▶ Truth #252: The Holy Ghost is saying that the renewal of the mind along with the regeneration and the reconciliation of the soul is as a trail to blaze through the uncharted thickets of carnality by the individual alone!

▶ Truth #253: Through a lifestyle of repentance, the saint can stand his ground on the basis of his saving faith in Christ and his compliance to the terms and the conditions of the word of God. In doing so, he will be able to stand against the heated violence that shall be applied to him by those opposed to God and His Christ!

▶ Truth #254: Whereas, Jesus Christ is described as our advocate, this furnace involves a cross examination process which purifies what we think we know by purging all bias and short sightedness, to reveal what we really don't know. What is left is the truth that we should know and it is this truth that shall set us free! Therefore, the Word of God is to the saint, as a defense attorney who cross examines him in court. In this, the word of His righteousness is also as this cross examination process to purify or qualify what faith he thinks he has, to reveal the faith he doesn't have and to teach him the faith that he should have and to expose the misunderstood faith he presently has!

▶ Truth #255: However, when self is denied through a lifestyle of repentance, and the cross of Christ is taken up, the devil and the host of Babylonian entities are overcome. In this, our personal property value is greatly increased!

▶ Truth #256: Through a lifestyle of repentance, the saint demonstrates by and through his audacious faith, that he is most precious in the sight of God and is of the highest value in his service towards Him!

▶ Truth #257: Therefore, what a furnace is to liquified metals, a kiln is to the progressive application of heat, so as to bring the object inserted, to a mature strength and durability!

Notes:

Addendum

The Utility and Application of Repentance: Freedom I, II and III

(Not all Inclusive)

- Addictions and Bondage
- Withdraw and Withdrawal Symptoms
- The Parasite of the Soul
- Freedom From Bondage
- The Head of the Bull is Carnal Mindedness
- Impression of Deception
- Till the Fallow Ground
- The Rejection of Bondage

- Agriculture and Horticulture
- The Proverb of the Shovel
- The Shovel Known as Repentance
- A Shovel Amoung Your Weapons
- The Fruit of Righteousness
- The Treader of Grapes and the Wine Press of God

- Aquatic and Nautical
- That Which is Deep is Known by He Who is Deeper Still
- Navy S.E.A.L.
- A Whale of a Time
- This Fish Represents Bondage and Bondage has Depth
- The Roots of the Mountains

- Mountains of Righteousness to Rise Above the Mountains of Carnality
  - Three Types of Mountains

- Brutishness (as the mindset of cattle mindedness, herd mentality, stupid, ignorant, foolish)
  - Carnal Attitudes and Hostile Mind Sets
  - Iniquity is to a Guilty Mind
  - Animal Impulses and Carnal Tendencies
  - Man's Carnality is the Scent Which the Dogs of Hell Follow
  - The Dogs of Hell

- Cardiology
- The Catered Heart
- The Parasite of the Soul
- The Heart of the Matter is Man's Carnality
- Blood Boiling Mad
- Getting Bloody in the Spirit

Complextion and Cosmetics
The Face of an Effeminent Man
A Method of Application
Playing the Harlot with Many Lovers
Make Thee Bald
Balderdash
The Balderdash of Repentance

Criminology and Jurisprudence
Heaven's Court
The Elements of Civil and Criminal Law
Iniquity is to a Guilty Mind
There's a Warrant Out for Your Arrest
Doing Time with Three Hots and Cot

FREEDOM III - Carnality, Denial and the Judgments of God

- A Prisoner of Jesus Christ
- The Evidence Speaks for Itself
- Turning State's Evidence
- Law Abiding Citizen
- The Law of Leprosy
- The Law of Repentance
- The House of Replies
- A Cell Within a Box
- Legal Claims
- To Judge is to Self Examine
- The Line of Righteous Judgement
- The Cirties of Refuge
- Jurisdiction
- Repentance as a Rod of Correction
- Habeas Corpus is a Demand to Bring that Man to Court
- A Mock Trial of David and Bathsheba
- The Duplicity of Judgement
- The Difference Between an Argument and a Debate
- The Finger Prints of Carnality
- Prisonization and Institutionlization

- Doctrine
- A Topical Investigation of Grace
- Age of Grace or the Age of Promiscuity
- The Nomenclature of Grace
- Contrasts to/of Grace
- The Seventh Day
- The Prophetic Word of Faith
- The Call of Repentance
- Noah Found Grace
- Repentance as a Memorial
- Repentance at the Tabernacle
- Repentance as the Knowledge of Salvation

FREEDOM III - Carnality, Denial and the Judgments of God

The Urim and Thummin

Domestic and Civil
An Elementary Presumption
Man's Traditional Precepts
A Crisis Intervention Technique
Entomology (study of insects)
The Cities of Refuge
The Cities of Refuge were not Permanent Abodes
Juridiction
The Duplicity of Judgement

Espionage and Sabotage
Repentance as the Rod of Correction
The Parasite of the Soul
Carnality as Another Gospel
Carnality as a Spy
The Booby Traps of Carnality
Carnality a a Concealed Weapon of Suicide

Freedom & Liberty
The Standard of Righteousness is the Flag of Faith
Righteousness as a Drill Instructor
A Call to Freedom
The Posterity of Bitternss According to NORAD
A Defense Code Against Carnality

Historical and Political
In League with our Lobbyist
A Tale of Two Cities
America's Ground Zero
America's Wake Up Call
Leprous America

Idolatry
To Appease the Gods
Fodder for the Gods

Infidelity and Unfaithfulness
Infidelity is Apostasy
What is Apostasy?
Spiritual Adultery
Cross Dressers and Switch Hitters are an Abomination

Immigration and Citizenship
The Cast System
The Kinsman Redeemer
The Skirts of the Vatican
The Cities of Refuge were not Permanent Abodes

Incarceration Instructions
Our Atonement is Our Involvement
The House of Replies
A Cell Within a Box
A Pisnoner of Jesu Christ
Doing Time with Three Hots and a Cot
There's a Warrant Out for Your Arrest
The Cities of Refuge

Judgement and Chastisement
I Abhor Myself in Dust and Ashes
Amend Your Ways
To Judge is to Self Examine
I Don't Know!

Metallurgy (metal working)
The Kiln of Repentance

The Furnace of Repentance
Chapter 40 The Seven FUrnances of Mystery Babylon

Military and War
Weapons of Mass Destruction
The Smoking Gun/Relic
A Shovel Amoung Your Weapons
Times of War Should Be Times of Reformation/Change
Pathology (as those things pertaining to a sick soul)
The Standard of Righteousness is the Flag of Faith
The Insignia of Righteousness
The Guidon
Righteousness as a Drill Instructor
Weapons of Judgement

National
A Tale of Two Cities
America's Ground Zero
America's Wake Up Call
Leprous America
We Have Ruined Our Country!

Necromancy (as those things pertaining to the dead)
The Death of the Wicked
The Death of the SaInt
A Bargain With Death
A National Funeral
Only Those on Death Row Know
Repentance as a Stay of Execution
Final Appeals for a Stay of Execution
Pangs of Death

Nutrition and Malnurishment

The Oil and the Wine
Progeny Means Fruit
Meat in God's House
Repentance s a Anti-histamine

Pathology (the science of the cause and effect of diseases)
The Parasite of the Soul
Carnal Bruising
Repentance as a Surgical Operation
The Spiritual Pathologist

Psychology
The Iniquity of Stubbornness
Foolishness is Carnality
Impressions of Deception
Carnal Knowledge is the Knowledge of Salvation

Reason & the Purpose
The Duplicity of Judgement
God's Purpose of/for Righteousness
The Purpose and Reason of and for Righteousness

Sanitation and Hygiene
Carnality, as Putting on the Dog
A Shovel Among Your Weapons
Mind Your Business
Carnality, the Land Mines of the Soul
God Does Not Want to Step in It
The Dung Smear
The Parasite of the Soul
Baring it All Means to Come Clean
Flies Are Drawn to Uncovered Food

Notes:

JUST RELEASED!
A NEW Song Single on CD
by Author & Prophetic Teacher Ed Marr

Direct from God's Heart to Yours "*Receive My Love*" is an open invitation for intimate fellowship from The Father to a lost and hurting America.

"The overwhelming sense of God's never-ending love for humanity comes through loud and clear. The inspired lyrics mixed with one of my favorite tunes, made me smile down on the inside."

– Aaron Jones, Missionary

Available at select Bookstores and
www.boldtruthpublishing.com

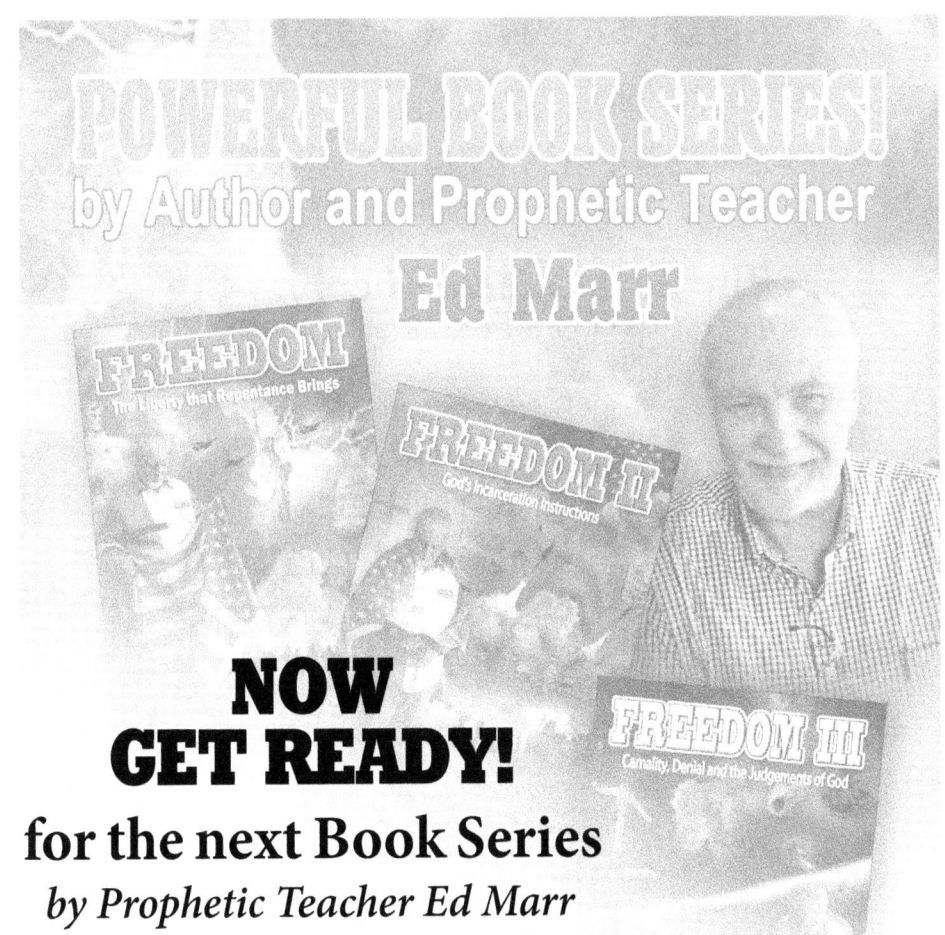

Check out these other Great Books from BOLD TRUTH PUBLISHING

by Adrienne Gottlieb

- **ISRAEL'S LEGITIMACY**
Why We Should Protect Israel At All Cost

- **The Replacement Theology LIE**
The Book Jews wished every Christian would read

-----

by Daryl Holloman

- **Seemed Good to The Holy Ghost**
Inspired Teachings by Brother Daryl
PLUS - Prophecies spoken in Pardo, Cebu, Philippines

- **The Adventures of Hezekiah Hare & Ernie Byrd**
A Children's Bible Adventure

- **Further Adventures**
More Good News as Hezekiah & Ernie follow Jesus.

-----

by Steve Young

- **SIX FEET DEEP**
Burying Your Past with Forgiveness

-----

by Paul Howard

- **THE FAITH WALK**
Keys to walking in VICTORY!

------

by Joe Waggnor

- **Bless THE KING**
Praise Poems for My Lord and Saviour

------

by Deborah K. Reed

- **THE GIFT of KNOWING Our Heavenly Father**
Abiding in Intimacy

by Jerry W. Hollenbeck
• The KINGDOM of GOD
An Agrarian Society
Featuring The Kingdom Realities, Bible Study Course,

• The Word of God
FATHER • WORD • SPIRIT
Literally THE WORD

-----

by Ed Marr
• C. H. P.
Coffee Has Priority
The Memoirs of a California Highway Patrol - Badge 9045

----

by Mary Ann England
• Women in Ministry
From her Teachings at the FCF Bible School - Tulsa, Oklahoma
(Foreword by Pat Harrison)

----

by James Jonsten
• WHO is GOD to YOU?
The path to know the most misunderstood name in the universe.

------

by Michael R. Hicks
• KINGDOM of LIGHT I / kingdom of Darkness
God's Word for Supernatural Healing, Deliverance and Protection

------

by Aaron Jones
• In the SECRET PLACE of THE MOST HIGH
Truth about Spritual Warfare

See more Books and all of our products at
www.BoldTruthPublishing.com

A MUST READ

Powerful testimony of what God did in, to, and through one State Traffic Officer.

"Action-packed, an intriguing mix of lawful AUTHORITY and Holy Ghost POWER. I thoroughly enjoyed it!"

- Pastor Kenn Watson
VICTORY Assembly of God

Available at select Bookstores and
www.boldtruthpublishing.com

www.ingramcontent.com/pod-product-compliance
Lightning Source LLC
Chambersburg PA
CBHW051906160426

43198CB00012B/1766